LET'S GO

"*Let's Go* illustrates how to create a winning culture that emphasizes growth by focusing on key values inherent to the type of team members a successful business looks to attract and develop. It outlines how to build a diverse workplace with a common culture that will lead to an increase in production, efficiency, loyalty, and ultimately growth. Anecdotes, real world examples, and his vast experience make this an easy read, applicable to any business model."

—Richard Shrouds, MD FAAP
Chief Medical Officer, Molina Healthcare of South Carolina

"Every company is like a living-being, with a DNA, a personality, and individual fingerprints. *Let's Go* is a refreshing focus on fundamentals in leadership and management using first-hand experiences to create a winning culture of healthy growth and purpose."

—LCDR Justin S. Brown, USN (Ret)
President and Founder, Blue Tide Aviation

T0004140

"With sharp perceptions and practical insights, Brent offers invaluable guidance for both aspiring stars just beginning their own journey as well as the seasoned business leaders. For anyone looking to thrive in today's dynamic business landscape, this book is an essential investment in yourself and your future development."

–Sterling Coker, MBA

Chief Revenue Cycle Officer, Mercy

"Adaptation and sustained growth, both personally and organizationally, can only occur when process is prioritized over outcome. A beautiful illustration of Receivable Solutions's 'north star,' in this book Brent Rollins presents a compelling description of the critical traits of the organization's team members, and the overarching organizational values, that keep RSi on course in their journey of process. After reading this book, it is very clear how Receivable Solutions remains steadfast in the perpetual pursuit of their theoretical limits while navigating the chaos inherent in growth."

–Peter L. Loper Jr., MD, MSEd, FAAP

Pediatrician, Psychiatrist, Child and Adolescent Psychiatrist

Founder and Principal, Pursuit Executive Leadership Coaching

LET'S GO

LET'S GO

HOW **CORE VALUES** AND **PURPOSE** CREATE A BUSINESS JOURNEY WORTH MAKING

BRENT D. ROLLINS

Advantage | Books

Published by Advantage Books, Charleston, South Carolina.
An imprint of Advantage Media.

ADVANTAGE is a registered trademark, and the Advantage colophon is a trademark of Advantage Media Group, Inc.

Printed in the United States of America.

10 9 8 7 6 5 4 3 2 1

ISBN: 978-1-64225-608-6 (Paperback)
ISBN: 978-1-64225-607-9 (eBook)

Library of Congress Control Number: 2023923058

Book design by Analisa Smith.

This publication is designed to provide accurate and authoritative information in regard to the subject matter covered. It is sold with the understanding that the publisher is not engaged in rendering legal, accounting, or other professional services. If legal advice or other expert assistance is required, the services of a competent professional person should be sought.

Advantage Books is an imprint of Advantage Media Group. Advantage Media helps busy entrepreneurs, CEOs, and leaders write and publish a book to grow their business and become the authority in their field. Advantage authors comprise an exclusive community of industry professionals, idea-makers, and thought leaders. For more information go to **advantagemedia.com**.

This book is dedicated to all the current, former, and future RSi teammates throughout the country and the incredible clients we have served together. It's been an amazing ride and we are just getting started.

CONTENTS

FOREWORD

W hen you hear the word artist, what image appears in your mind?

A painter? Sculptor? Poet? Actor? Musician?

No matter the image, I feel safe assuming our minds wouldn't immediately conjure a picture of a business setting. However, when Brent asked me to write the foreword for *Let's Go*, I repeatedly returned to that word: artist.

In his book *The Icarus Deception*, Seth Godin describes artists as those who are "seizing new ground, making connections between people or ideas, working without a map—these are works of art, and if you do them, you are an artist, regardless of whether you wear a smock, use a computer, or work with others all day long."

Seizing new ground. Connecting people and ideas. Not merely working without a map but creating it.

In my fifteen years working with Brent, including the last seven at RSi, I can't think of a better trilogy of actions to describe his work. Scratch that, his *art*.

All great artists possess two complementary skills: aggregation and application.

They aggregate teaching, lessons, and stories of both the inspirational and informational variety. They apply that acquired knowledge into consistent practice.

Aggregation is how artists seize new ground and ideas. Application is how artists connect people to those ideas.

Brent's discipline as an aggregator is unparalleled, and his uniqueness in this area begins with his intentional avoidance of everyday distractions. He does not participate in any form of social media and is less tethered to the smartphone dopamine dispenser than most of us. His primary input is reading, and through physical books (I've unsuccessfully tried to sell him on a Kindle for years), podcasts, and Audible, Brent's media consumption is curated around improving as a person and leader.

His application in setting our vision, values, and culture is intentional without being narrow, confident without being arrogant, and presented from a student's mind with the heart of a teacher. Through this, he has fostered an atmosphere of optimism and celebration at RSi.

When our results exceed expectations, we celebrate. When we individually or collectively fall on our faces, we celebrate because we know we will learn something new about ourselves.

What Brent has compiled in *Let's Go* isn't your typical business book. It's a nine-year snapshot of a still unfinished work. His lifelong pursuit of the artistry of leadership shines as he illustrates the principles that shaped our DNA, Core Values, and Purpose while being an engaging storyteller throughout.

I can attest the concepts within are lived out daily and continually challenge our entire team to iterate and improve upon them. They have been the cornerstones of the most fruitful seven years of my career, and I know they can do the same in yours.

–DUSTIN SPENCER

Chief Sales Officer | RSi RCM

INTRODUCTION

There are two types of people in the world. Those that are humble and those that are about to be.

—CLINT HURDLE, FORMER MANAGER OF THE COLORADO ROCKIES

On my first day at Receivable Solutions (RSi), LLC—April 1, 2014—I walked into the office early. I'm supposed to be there at 7:45, but around 7:15, I showed up and walked through the doors. Nobody was there except who I thought was the cleaning crew.

I found the restroom by following the smell of bleach, walked in, and saw two guys there cleaning the bathroom, so I introduced myself. "Hey, it's my first day here. I appreciate you guys cleaning up. Do you know when the staff will get here?"

The response I got was funny. They both looked at each other and said, "You know, we're here. We are staff. We work here."

It took me aback a little. I mean, what company has their employees doing the work of a janitorial service? But I recovered.

"That's great. Can I get your names?"

They introduced themselves. I filed their names away somewhere in the recesses of my brain, politely excused myself, and went on to where I think my office is located.

Soon the owners popped in; we talked and enjoyed a good conversation. I told them my plan for the day, met the management team and individual reps, and then went from there. Next, we all went out, and they introduced me to the entire staff, which, back then, were less than forty people. Once that was done, I returned to my office to start my day.

I went through a list of the management team, and I started bringing them in, one by one. As I talked to each person, I asked them, "Who runs this operation?"

They each replied, "Well, that's Bob; he's second in command."

I also heard, "That's Lee. He's your guy."

OK, great. I'll talk to them last, I thought to myself.

After a full afternoon of conducting these interviews, I finally get to the end, and Lee walks through the door. Lo and behold, he was one of the guys cleaning up the bathroom that morning.

We had a great meeting, and Lee is still with the company today. He was there five years at that point, bringing his tenure up to, at the time of this writing, roughly fourteen years.

Finally, it was Bob, who also was moonlighting as a janitor with Lee earlier in the day. As it turns out, back then he was the interim operations manager, which made it even more shocking to me that he would be cleaning bathrooms before his workday began. (He's now vice president [VP] of operations.) We had a great conversation, riffing on what's going to happen next, what's the growth plan, and all that. We hit it off and started making big plans.

"What if this?" "What could happen if we tried that?" and so on. We put all that on a whiteboard that hangs in my office today, with the thought that, *Man, if everything goes right…*

This brainstorming session became the basis for our plans moving forward. We always focused on two numbers: one for revenue and the other for profit, as stated in earnings before interest, taxes, depreciation, and amortization (EBITDA). Then, in creating our list, we put down at least fifty items that we wanted to do. This included everything from T-shirts to parties and everything in between. We were a tremendously small company back then—again, not even forty employees—and we didn't have a lot of benefits. By doing some other small things, including expanded vacation days and increasing pay rates, we could close that gap. We took all those ideas, wrote them down, and then took a picture of the board. After we tallied up our notes, we had over seventy-five things we wanted to do.

With everything now written down, we wanted to put some numbers on the board as well. The big goal was for revenue to be $100 million, the EBITDA $40 million, and total employee count to be around 750. As it stands today, we're well on our way.

That whiteboard became critical. We would have it handy in meetings and refer to it constantly. When it came time to move, we carefully took the whiteboard with us, making sure we didn't erase anything, and hung it up in our conference room so that everyone could see the numbers themselves.

I had big plans on that first day in 2014, and by the time the sun went down, things were different from what I had imagined. But now I get to go into work every day excited to see what lies in front of me. And that's a pretty great feeling to have.

. . . .

RSi RCM is a receivables management company, servicing hospitals and large medical providers across the United States. We're primarily a call center operation, where our teammates work with insurance companies and consumers to recover funds for the healthcare providers we serve. The two founders of the company previously worked at hospitals and were clients of mine in the mid-1990s. Decades later, when their company was much smaller and they wanted to grow, they reached out to see how we all could work together.

The owners were great guys and cagey businesspeople who were prepared to put forth all of the resources necessary to ensure that growth happened. The timing was right, too. I was ready to leave the position I had been in for twenty-two years and eager to try some different ideas at a new company. Sometimes, things just work out.

Now, nine years since I first started, as the CEO of RSi, I've learned a lot that I would like to share with all of you, which is why I decided to write it all down.

Let's take a moment to break down this book. Over the next few chapters, I'm going to start out explaining what we look for in employees, as well as the importance of core values for an organization like ours. Then I will explain what each of those values are, laying them out in clear and simple terms.

Now I love stories, and so each chapter begins with a story. Sometimes they're fables; tales that you may have heard over the years in one form or another. Others are actual stories of real-life events, with just the names changed for obvious reasons. I even pepper a few of these events through the chapters themselves to illustrate my points.

See, it's easy to read a book about company values and then shrug them off as something that could've been condensed into a post on LinkedIn. That's why, for me, it helps to see these things in practice. To show how when a problem occurs, leaning back on yourself and your company's values can truly help move you forward.

By the time you're done, you'll be able to take away quite a few things from the book, but it all depends on your perspective. From my end, I see this as a training manual for future RSi teammates as well as a guideline for future leaders of industry. But for you, well, it could mean a lot of things. If you're starting a company, here's your values handbook—or at least a good place to start. And if you're just a regular Joe or Jane who wants to understand a bit more about the business world, we've got some info for you as well. There's something here for most everyone.

Enjoy yourself. I don't take myself too seriously, and there are no really deep concepts here. It's just a basic, direct, organic overview of core values and how they can steer a team to success.

CHAPTER ONE

DNA

. . . .

Be who you say you are. Do what you say you will do.

−JAMES M. KOUZES

Let me tell you a quick story about a farmer and a snake. Skip this part if you've heard this one before.

There was a farmer who lived in a small village, and he was known as having a super kind and generous soul. He was the type of guy who would pick you up at the airport—even during rush hour. Anyways, one day he was walking through his fields, and he found a snake that was injured. Now he couldn't just let this thing go and die on its own; he needed to tend to its wounds. So, very carefully, the farmer picked up the snake and delicately carried it back to its house.

It took some time, but the farmer, with all of his love and devotion, took care of and tended to the snake's wounds. Eventually, the snake got better, and the farmer returned it to its fields so that the reptile could live out its days.

Life goes on, and the farmer did what he did on a regular basis. Until one day, as he's working the fields, he sees the snake again. That's when the snake hissed and said, "I'm going to bite you!"

Now seeing a snake slithering up to you in an attacking position is pretty scary on its own, but now that same snake can talk? This obviously threw the farmer for a loop, but it also raised more questions than he had answers. So he asked him.

"Why would you do that?" asked the farmer. "I saved your life!"

The snake responded as you might imagine a snake to respond: "It's in my nature to bite. I can't help it."

The farmer heard the snake, thought about it for a brief moment, and then sighed. "I may have saved your life, but I can't change your nature." And with that, the farmer turned around and walked away, leaving the snake to do its thing, which, according to the animal, was biting things.

I say this to explain a simple thing that we all may have observed over the years. While you can do all you want to help train a teammate and get them to be the best person they can be, ultimately you can't often change their nature and behavior. Put simply, a snake's gonna be a snake, and if we expect otherwise, we're going to get bitten.

That's why DNA is such an important concept to us. Of course, we're not totally using it in the way you might expect, so let's dive a little bit deeper into the concept.

Defining DNA

Unless they're in their late teens, everybody who shows up to work here at RSi has probably had a job somewhere else at some point in their lives. Why did they leave that other company? Was it for better pay? More vacation time? More prestige? Bad management? There are a million reasons why someone leaves their place of employment, and we didn't want to fall into a lot of those traps.

Now some things are impossible to avoid, and we get that. But when we started thinking about things like our company values, we decided instead to begin with a basic premise: we wanted to have people who actually wanted to work for us. They desired the kind of work environment we offered, with fun people and the common goal of delivering great results.

That's not easy to find, and it can be a struggle to get in large numbers for sure.

Through the years at RSi, many leaders, teammates, and even the original owners wanted us to sit down and come up with a mission statement. A reasonable request and a noble goal for some companies. For us, we didn't need that—not yet, at least. Instead, we wanted to define the DNA of our company: traits that would tell ourselves and the world who we really are at our core.

If you've watched a procedural crime drama or watched a movie about dinosaurs walking around in the 1990s, you've heard of DNA. It's the building block of life, the double-helix chain of information that makes us, human beings, what we are. RSi didn't need a mission statement; we needed to describe exactly who the people were who worked at our company.

We started with that DNA and determined we wanted people who are sharp, committed, and enthusiastic. We also wanted that commitment to be bidirectional; we, the leadership, would contain those same traits and behaviors.

So how did we get those kinds of people on board and involved? By first defining what each of those terms means.

Sharp

You've known somebody who's sharp before. Maybe you're sharp yourself. And on the surface, being sharp is a pretty straightforward concept, but I'll just share RSi's "formal definition."

"Sharp" describes a teammate's ability to think quickly, adapt to new situations, and solve problems creatively.

Now that's all well and good, but what does that *actually* mean? Well, let's break it down even further.

Thinking quickly is not a learned skill. It's something you can either do or not do. There's not a lot of in-between there, not really. These are the people who, when confronted with a decision, are able to make the call in the heat of the moment rather than hem and haw about the whole thing.

Now this doesn't mean they make rash decisions. They do not just rush into things, head down, ready to tackle whatever lies in front of them; they're able to quickly process the stakes and make an informed decision in a short period of time.

Let me give you an example of a friend of mine from way back. Remember the iPod? Well, at one time there was the iPod Photo, and it was a big deal because not only did it have a color screen, but it also could store your photos. I know, the mid-2000s were a crazy time.

Anyways, my friend wanted to get one. But it was $300, and that was a lot of money for him. This would be his first digital media player, and he wanted to make sure it would last a long time. Was this the right call? He just wasn't sure.

Boy, did he debate the issue. It was weeks, maybe months, that he waited to make that call, and eventually me and everyone else he spoke to was tired of hearing about it. His girlfriend ended up saying to him, "Just buy the damn iPod and shut up about it." So buy it he did, and yes, he was very happy with the purchase.

But that's not quick thinking. In his case, that was more procrastination than anything else. What we want is not quite the opposite, but somewhere in between.

Now why is thinking quickly important? There are lots of times, particularly in the healthcare-revenue-cycle-management world (not really as boring as it sounds—I promise!), where a question is posed, and you need to have an answer. You cannot keep a patient, payer, or consumer waiting. Ever. If you're going to "iPod Photo" the thing, then you'll never make a decision, and you'll lose the person on the other end of the line. But, if you can think quickly, then you'll be able to address the issue and respond appropriately. That's what we're looking for—sharp.

Let's address the next aspect of our definition of sharp, which is the ability to adapt to new situations. RSi isn't going to throw you to the wolves and expect you to fight your way out—not right off the bat, anyway. But there will be situations where you find yourself in new territory. Maybe it's as simple as a promotion you've earned, or possibly you're just dealing with a different client and everything has changed. Whatever the scenario, we want you to be able to figure out what's going on yourself and then navigate the challenges appropriately.

That also means you'll need to have the third part of our sharp definition handled as well: solving problems creatively.

The phrase, "thinking outside of the box," is tired and way overused in pretty much all forms of media, and there's a reason for that. All companies need their employees to be able to react quickly to changing circumstances and then find solutions to complex problems. This does often require thinking outside of your normal zone of comfort, which, naturally, makes some people, well, uncomfortable.

But that's what we want to push. Our teammates are intelligent and insightful, and can make informed decisions under pressure. Why? Because they have solid analytical skills. They can look at a scenario and see the patterns, trends, and anomalies that are going to shape their decision-making process. It's these skills that make us stronger as a company and individuals stronger on their respective teams.

Basically, we want people who are sharp because they're essential to the team. They help us identify new opportunities, streamline processes, and keep us ahead of the competition. Being sharp is in the DNA of every associate here at RSi, as well as the ones who are coming up next.

Enthusiastic

Now when it comes to enthusiasm, it's really all about passion. People on our staff are, first and foremost, passionate about their work. And that's just where things get rolling.

You probably heard the old saying growing up: do something you love, and you'll never work a day in your life. And while that may be true for some people, that's definitely not the case for everyone. Fact is, some of us get a job just to survive, or maybe because we show some kind of aptitude in a particular area and feel compelled to move in that direction.

This puts us in a bit of a conundrum here. We want people who are passionate about what they do, but ultimately, there's a limited number of people out there who do exactly what RSi does already.

So let's expand things out a bit. We want people who are enthusiastic, yes. And definitely passionate about what they do, sure. But can you come to RSi with no experience in our work and still fill this qualification? Absolutely.

See, being passionate about what you do doesn't have to limit you to a particular vocation. If your job is filling potholes, first off, you're doing amazing work, and my rims and tires thank you. But let's say you want to move out of the asphalt industry and do something over here with us. We're good with that—just show the same passion for your work here as you did with fixing road damage. While enthusiasm does not automatically include being an expert in a particular field, and we understand that, we know it is a critical quality all of our employees need to possess.

That's because an enthusiastic employee goes above and beyond to ensure the success of everyone on their team and the organization as a whole. They're motivated, positive about now, and, arguably more importantly, optimistic about the future. As a result, they are very dedicated to their work and what they do, and they take pride in their achievements. As we say, hire for DNA, train for skill.

Every company wants enthusiastic employees like that on their team, because it lifts everyone up. Ever been at a job where you've had a real Larry Lowmood in the group? That one guy who never stops complaining about how corporate won't listen to him, or the woman who will tell anyone within earshot how she doesn't trust the CEO for one reason or another. It sucks. You end up not wanting to head into the office for fear of getting trapped by one of those negative people at the water cooler.

Enthusiastic employees change that equation. They inspire others to succeed and are just critical to RSi's success. It's like they're injecting morale into every employee every morning, and that's a real winner for all involved. It increases productivity and helps foster the culture of success that we want here.

Committed

The last one in the big three is being committed. Here, we want a teammate who is not only dedicated to us and our cause but also has a solid work ethic and is reliable. But let's dive a little bit deeper.

We all probably worked at a place when we were teenagers. Maybe we didn't have a strong commitment to the company or what they stood for, and it was easy enough to "check out" whenever we were doing work. We were earning a paycheck, sure. But we certainly didn't go above and beyond.

Being dedicated to a company and their cause is important for both parties. On your end, if you truly believe in what your company does, it means you're not forcing yourself to get out of bed every day. You want the company to succeed, because it aligns with your own values. It creates such a different dynamic every day for everyone involved, and we definitely value that.

A solid work ethic is important at every job, but it's not always one that people quite understand. It means that you, as an employee, value work as a concept. You attach a certain amount of self-worth to what you do for a job and that by working hard you will achieve the results you desire.

We've all known people with a horrible work ethic. They're the people who, like the teenager in the example above, checked out at one point or another. You know the type. Like the checkout person at your local big-box store who can hardly be bothered to look you in the eyes while they scan your goods. That's not who we're looking for. No, we want the people who are driven to do their work and take pride in doing it well.

Now, I say all this knowing that it probably gets a pretty heavy eye roll from some people, and I get that. "Of *course* a company wants to hire people with a good work ethic. In other news: Water is wet." But what I'm saying is actually a little bit different.

When people look for a job, they usually try to find a place that meets their criteria. That could include commute times, salary, benefits, and a dozen other qualifications. But at some point, they start to think about what the company does and how they fit into that equation. They want to work for someone who has similar values to their own (including work ethic), because that way they will fit in better.

When an employee shares the values of their employer, a true bond forms. They both have the same mission; therefore, one's success is also the other's. This creates not only loyalty but also motivation. And when you push forward on those two issues, you see how that brings everybody up. A rising tide lifts all ships, right?

People who are committed are the backbone of our organization. They're the ones who provide the reliability and stability that we—and every other company—rely on for success. Their commitment helps us all succeed, and that is why that particular trait is part of our DNA.

And That's Not All

Now look, it's great to talk about our core traits and all that, but let's be clear, these are not the only things that we're looking for. Some people may have strands of our DNA built into their own, but it can take more time on the team to bring them out. And that's totally fine; we get it. But there are other things we look for as well that don't seem as flashy right off the bat.

We place a high value on diversity and inclusivity. We want a very diverse workforce for a number of reasons. If our team were made up of people who all had the same background, came from the same place, and thought the same basic things, then we would all likely share the same perspective. That's bad for the organization. It means we have blind spots that people of other genders, backgrounds, and races may not have. A single viewpoint quickly leads to a total inability to adapt.

Those different perspectives drive companies forward. This isn't about politics or positioning. For us, what we have learned over the years is that a diverse and inclusive team is simply a better team. One that can have fun together, compete at the highest level, and win consistently. That's why it's so important we continue to follow those principles.

We also want our employees to exhibit a willingness to learn and grow. This doesn't seem like too much of a stretch; I think most people want to improve themselves as they get older. But there are the occasional folks that you run into who don't have any motivation to improve their standing. They're fine working where they are, how they are, forever.

Good example: A friend of mine's wife worked at a pharmacy right out of high school. She stayed there for twenty years, and, while she did get promoted, it wasn't because she tried. She never made it to manager or anything like that and still made hourly wages until she was laid off in 2022.

Now let me be clear, there is nothing wrong with what she was doing, because she did exhibit a willingness to learn and grow—she just didn't do it at her job. Her goal was to travel and learn about the world as much as possible, which meant spending as little time at work as she could. But that's not what we're looking for. We absolutely encourage interests outside of our organization while at the same time wanting people who push to learn and grow within their job, because they value what they do for eight-ish hours a day. People can and do succeed with regularity at RSi, and for that to truly work, they need to want to learn, grow, and develop at every opportunity.

There are other more intangible traits we desire in an employee, but ultimately, the combination of everything results in a workforce that is dynamic, innovative, and capable of achieving its goals. That's really what we want; the total picture, as it were.

Now all that said, we know we're looking for a lot, and that's OK. I suppose the point here is we want to hit the highest and best combination of traits that we have in our DNA to match with an employee who will truly succeed and have fun doing it. When we get that equation worked out, the results can be truly spectacular.

The Importance of DNA

Now all this is well and good, but let's go back to why we place such an emphasis on determining the DNA of our company?

Because of what I do, I spend a lot of time on planes. And since I'm on the East Coast, I find myself going for five-plus-hour jaunts, sometimes just for the day. In most cases, a typical week will include ten-plus hours of plane time at a minimum.

One tremendous benefit of all this time in the air? I have the amazing opportunity to read a lot of books. One of my favorites is *Recruit Rockstars: The 10 Step Playbook to Find the Winners and Ignite Your Business* by Jeff Hyman. It is as practical and insightful as any book relating to staffing I've read. In it, Hyman argues that the DNA of your employees is crucial to your organization's success. That finding and hiring employees with the right cultural fit, values, and work ethic is just as important as their skills and experience. And when you do just that, you get this culture that's unstoppable and fosters serious growth and success. It's pretty powerful stuff. Again, it's a version of hire for DNA and train for skill.

Conversely, if you should decide to ignore those traits and how they fit with what exists in your organization, the toxic work environment you'll unwittingly create will be a disaster and could push back any progress you could make.

Now when we were a smaller company, none of this was a real issue. It's easier to manage company culture when there are a few dozen people working within arm's reach of one another. We all had a sense of shared purpose back then. It was simple. Fun, but simple.

But now, as we have over six hundred employees on staff, it's more difficult to get that culture going and thriving. Sometimes you bring on new people, and they just don't care about the company's values and cultures. For them, it's just a paycheck, so why put forth the effort? And when you get too many people like that in the system, it becomes difficult to achieve all of your goals as a company.

Reading that book, therefore, was enlightening. It validated something we were seeing in the real world and wasn't just some crazy theory by someone who wanted to sell some paperbacks. If we wanted to change, we needed to adjust our culture and our hiring process. In addition to seeing if someone was qualified for a job, we had to figure out if they were qualified and fit within the company's culture and values. It narrowed our talent pool quite a bit—would it be worth it?

Our quick answer? Absolutely. We realized right away this was a win for us. Once we had the right people working at the company, the cultural continuity started building. Now, when new employees start, the existing ones become ambassadors for our DNA, and that helps us all on board the new hires so they fit in just as well. It becomes like a perpetual motion machine, continually pushing the group forward as a whole. It's spectacular to see it in action.

This also helps foster a sense of collaboration and shared purpose with everyone on the team. Now think about that for a second. If the entire staff shares the same ideals, then they all want the company to grow and thrive. There's no one team or person who gets the benefits of success, and instead we all share in it together. We work more effectively because we're all pushing forward toward the same path.

I'm so glad I read Hyman's book on that flight, because it helped take our company culture to another level. Once you're done reading this book, pick up his. It's a great read and well worth your time.

STUFF WORTH REMEMBERING

Just like the DNA of your body defines who you become physically, the DNA of a company defines what your business is. The difference is you can't change the DNA of your body, but you can for your business.

A huge part of the DNA of your company is your employees—arguably the biggest portion. Of course, I'm mixing metaphors a bit here, but the idea is you need your people to share a common goal with your business and believe in what you do. It's how you take your operations from average to good to excellent and then to elite.

It's critical you establish what you want your company to be and how it functions early. And if for some reason you're late to the party, get onto it now. This will help you shape your company in the right direction and ensure that future team members share your vision.

Check in on your DNA regularly, too. Is your company constructed the way you want? If not, check those building blocks first.

Tips to Check In on Your Company's DNA

1. Come up with at least three traits that you consider essential parts of your company's DNA. Choosing an attitude, a behavior, and an aptitude will get you started.

2. Examine the DNA of your company as it stands, and write down what needs to change to match your ideal scenario.

3. Get clear on the building blocks you want in every new teammate.

CHAPTER TWO

THE IMPORTANCE OF VALUES

If someone shows you what they value, believe them.

—DUSTIN SPENCER

O n an episode of the podcast *Decoder*, hosted by Nilay Patel of The Verge, Brian Chesky, the CEO of Airbnb, told a story of a problem that almost sunk the company[1].

For those of you who don't know, Airbnb is based on the concept of a bed and breakfast. These are hotel-like places where people can spend the night in what appears to be a regular home. Airbnb's concept meant that regular folks like you and me could rent out a

---

1   Nilay Patel, "'I Can't Make Products Just for 41-Year-Old Tech Founders': Airbnb CEO Brian Chesky Is Taking It Back to Basics," The Verge, May 9, 2023, https://www.theverge.com/2023/5/9/23716903/ airbnb-ceo-brian-chesky-rooms-ai-travel-future-of-work-summer-2023.

room, a shed, or even our entire house to some fine person on the internet and make some extra money. On the other side of things, travelers like myself could go to one of these places to stay when we're out on a trip and maybe get some more freedom or variety than your traditional hotel.

But back in 2011, when Airbnb was still pretty small, they had a major problem. They had a host in San Francisco named EJ who hosted a guest who destroyed their apartment. This was a big problem; if Airbnb hosts couldn't trust their guests, then there was no reason for them to rent out their rooms. But by the time Chesky heard about the problem, he thought it was resolved and even wrote an article on *TechCrunch* about this issue proclaiming victory. Problem was that wasn't actually the case.

No, EJ fired back, explaining things were very much an issue, and the problem grew from there. Every time Chesky tried to defend the company and solve the problem, things got worse. They hired a crisis management firm to try to solve the issue, but it didn't work, either.

"And at this point, I came to a conclusion that the most important decision I'm going to make would be based on principles, not on outcomes," Chesky said. "In other words, I was going to make principle decisions, not business decisions. And the principle decision is: If I can't figure out the outcome, how do I want to be remembered?"

So he did something both crazy and unique for the CEO of a start-up: he apologized.

At the time, Airbnb had a $5,000 guarantee for hosts, meaning they would be covered up to $5,000 for incidents like what happened to EJ. But now he bumped it up to $50,000 and applied it retroactively to all past incidents as well. It was pretty nuts—and it worked. His company continued to grow and created an entirely new lodging category.

When the COVID-19 pandemic hit almost a decade later, he came up with a plan, again.

"And in this board meeting, I wrote out a series of principles about how to manage the crisis," he said. "And the first principle I set is we're going to act decisively. The second is we're going to preserve cash. The third is we're going to act with shareholders in mind. And the fourth is we're going to win the next travel season."

He continues: "And I had even more detailed principles, and I said to the board, 'I'm going to have to make like a thousand decisions a week, and so I can't run every decision by you. So instead, let's agree on the principles, and I'll use those principles to make these decisions.'"

Do you see what he did there? He knew that if he were to ask for permission every time, he would get slowed down, and the company could stumble. But if everyone agreed on how he would make decisions, then he was free to make them without asking first.

These principles helped shape what Airbnb is today and where it will be moving forward. They're now critical to the company, and while they may change for various reasons, they are their North Star.

Are values important? Absolutely. Now let's dig into more about why.

It's Who We Are

Values aren't always very high on the priority list when you start a business. After all, you're usually running around trying to figure out how to get the coffee machine working while simultaneously closing a deal to bring in some money to keep the business going. But creating them, no matter how long it takes, is important, particularly as you grow and expand. Because ultimately, your values are part of your identity. They're who you are as a business, and that's kind of a big deal.

Let's touch back to that Airbnb story. The values that we have are going to inform our decision-making, our behavior, our actions, and everything else. Use whatever metaphor you like; values are the lamps to light your way, maps to guide you, or the trail of breadcrumbs that take you out of the forest. No matter what you do, those values are what make you and your company, *you*.

But here's the other thing: Those values you're practicing? They are also creating your culture. Basically, we can say that if you're going to work here, you're going to live by these values. And while that may sound harsh, or rigid, or unreasonable, these values are the foundation of everything else we want to be and become as an organization. Everyone makes the effort to live them out. (Note: Making the effort is key here. We realize none of us perfectly adhere to all of our values all the time.)

To be clear, we're obviously not the only ones who feel the importance of values in an organization, especially a growing business. The other day I was visiting a friend in the hospital and right there, right as I walked past the front desk, were the hospital's values in big, gold letters. I imagine most folks don't give that sign more than a glance, but I sure did take a moment to see what they were working with. While it would take time and experience to see if they are truly living those values, I at least know their targets.

By the way, this commitment to our values is bidirectional. We're committed to these values in our treatment of our employees, and we expect that commitment in return. We'll hold up things on our end, and you should do the same. In that way, things will all work out for the better.

We often say our core values are not aspirational. In other words, if it's who we truly are, then we should have awareness of where we might deviate from them, but we should not have to change.

Trust the Process

A quick history lesson and how our core values were codified. With the DNA of our company now defined, it was time to move forward into determining the company's values. You might think that would be a pretty straightforward process, but it was a bit more convoluted than that.

In my case, I started by reading several books about how to define your core values. But one thing that I read repeatedly that really stuck with me the most was to identify what you're doing now that works.

It's an interesting idea and one that can only ever really happen if you're actively running a company; doing that before you sign your articles of incorporation documents doesn't help. And so, with all that in mind, we started thinking about what things we were doing now that worked, and the first one that hit me was about the truth.

It occurred to me that when I ask someone a question, I'm getting an answer. People here didn't hide or couch their answers behind fancy language. No, they were straight shooters all the way. Honest and direct was the course of the day, combined with frank and sincere feedback. So what does that mean? Well, after consulting the thesaurus for options, it meant we were practicing candor, and we had just done a session at our office on that very topic just the week before. Boom. Candor was going to be one of our company values.

Now we were picking up steam. Next we put the entire executive team in a room and started brainstorming further. One of the first questions asked was, "What word describes us better than anything else?"

Our chief sales officer said, "That's easy. Growth."

He was 100 percent correct. We want to grow in everything we do. Boom, there's number two. Next up is how we're constantly telling people, "Hey, we're not winning as individuals here. We've got to win as teams." It turns out that can be parlayed quite nicely into Team over Individual. After all, one person can't be a football team.

So while Growth and Candor came pretty easily, the next few were a little bit harder to come by. We knew what kind of environment we had: high energy, fun, and cooperative. We also knew the type of environment we wanted to avoid: whining, grumbling, and criticizing. So when we stumbled on No BCD—blaming, complaining, and defending—we knew it was absolutely perfect for RSi. Now, the idea of No BCD is not exclusive to us; it's from a guy named Tim Kight who runs a company named Focus 3. Consuming just a little of his material, we all agreed, "We have to adopt this one. It describes us."

With those out of the way, we started thinking about logistics. We realized that one of our core values had to speak about the way we spend our money. Without that, we're being disingenuous. That's where No Return on Investment (ROI), No Spend came from.

But now that all or most of the values were in place, we had to decide what to do with them. Do we hang them up on the wall? Give them out in a pamphlet? No. Actually our first idea when it came to using our values was a bit counterintuitive.

Don't Just Pay Lip Service

When you've got a bunch of people sitting in a room and deciding on company values, you'd think the next step would be pretty straightforward. First you'd bring a designer and copywriter into the fold, and have them design some cool posters and merch to fit with those themes. Then we'd have a big event, showcasing all of the signage we put up all over the office with our new company values and give away some free T-shirts or mugs. And from that point forward, you couldn't walk twenty feet without hitting some kind of message about RSi's values. After all, that's what most other companies would do, right?

Yeah, that's not us. In fact, we made it a point to *not* write them down. Ever.

Unless it's in a book, obviously. (And yes, I understand the irony.)

No, we didn't want posters in the break room or sitting on a sticky note on someone's monitor. We had to *live* these values. And once we did that, we would never have to write them down because they were just a part of who we are.

That's, of course, easy to say, and yet somehow we've figured it out. The creation (more like the identification) of our values was done in just a few meetings, but once we had them sorted out, it became all about word of mouth and our actions. We would hold meetings introducing the concepts to our other team members, sure. But the main thing was for leadership to show how we practiced these values. We're not just paying lip service to our core values; we actually *live* them.

That's both easy and difficult to do. Arguably the easiest one to perform was candor. By practicing that regularly, other team members started to see that we weren't all just talking out of our rear ends. We meant what we said, and for some people, that was revolutionary.

Sometimes showing our values meant pointing that out during the decision-making process. That would point out not only something like our growth value but also candor.

But values, like anything else, also need other components to keep us moving. And in our case, that was purpose.

Stoicism and Virtues

Over one thousand years ago, stoic philosophers dealt with the same problems we face today. Sure, they didn't have smartphones constantly showing them the latest trends, but they did have things like jobs, desires, questions about what happens after death, and many of the other primordial things that we all think about.

Stoicism, as a philosophy, takes a lot of those issues head-on, and while it's a complex topic that covers a wide variety of different things, one issue they did discuss regularly were values, specifically, the four virtues:

- courage
- justice
- temperance
- wisdom

If you want to dive into stoic philosophy—and I recommend that you do—the most approachable modern-day writer on this topic is Ryan Holiday. He's written books about stoicism for several years now, including *Ego Is the Enemy*, *The Obstacle Is the Way*, and *Lives of the Stoics*, to name just a few. These books are easy and quick reads, propelling you through historical tales and applying them to everyday events.

Holiday writes about this stuff all the time, pretty much everywhere you can think of, including this piece on *Business Insider* about those four virtues:

> They are the most essential values in stoicism. "If, at some point in your life," Marcus Aurelius wrote, "you should come across anything better than justice, truth, self-control, courage—it must be an extraordinary thing indeed." That

was almost twenty centuries ago. We have discovered a lot of things since then—automobiles, the internet, cures for diseases that were previously a death sentence—but have we found anything better?[2]

Now I'm not a stoic philosopher, nor do I think I ever will become one at this point. But for me, the big takeaway here is the importance of having values in general. Not everyone has them, and neither does every company. But once you do have some sense of what your values are, you can push forward on everything else—company initiatives, bold ideas, and all anything else. Really, the core values are the foundation of your organization, and you have to build that part first before you stack things on top.

Like the stoics, these values are designed to give you guidance when you're lost in the darkness. A path to follow when nothing else is visible. These are your tenets, and if you truly believe in them, following those rules will never let you down. They frame your thinking and guide nearly all your decisions. When in doubt, consult the core values. They provide the same clear direction for everyone on the team.

Whether or not you believe in our company's values is up to you, and opinions are what they are. But their mere existence is a sign that we do care about our people and what they do—so much so that we're going to give them a clear and concise road map to succeed.

---

2   Ryan Holiday, "7 Things the Ancient Stoics Can Teach You about Becoming a Strong, Happy, and Morally Sound Professional," Business Insider, September 15, 2020, https://www.businessinsider.com/lessons-from-ancient-stoics-on-morality-success-and-happiness-2020-9.

The Purpose

Not to get all deep and philosophical here, but I like to think that we all have a purpose. Our purpose gives us a reason for being, as it were; why we get up in the morning and do whatever it is we do.

Why would you pick a purpose? There are lots of reasons, but ultimately it's so that when you find yourself at a crossroads and need to determine which way to go, follow your purpose, and you'll always end up on the right path.

We have to face difficult decisions all the time here at RSi, and sometimes that means boiling things down to brass tacks. It helps a ton to have a purpose, and while not every business needs one, it certainly doesn't hurt.

Oh, I should probably mention what ours is, anyway:

To create a workplace where team members can have fun, grow together, and deliver outstanding results to those we serve.

So how did we get there? Well, as you can imagine, we started by looking at other companies' purpose statements, and none of them felt right for a number of reasons. The main reason was because we felt like copying another company's purpose statement was pointless. Instead, we started thinking about what we wanted to become as a company—what we want to do and how we want to move forward.

Soon, we realized that our purpose came down to the people. We want to enjoy working with the folks we see every day, whether we come into the office virtually or not. For us, our purpose is the people and the place where we work, and although there is a component about results, it's not the only focus. We knew then and know now, if we get the right people having a great time in an engaging environment, we will generate incredible results.

Now you may find yourself seeing different results in your own life and work. Heck, we've had a few people look at our purpose and question it. "It should be more about the business. It should be more about what you do in the marketplace." For us, this is amazing. It tells us, whether we're hearing from a current teammate, a candidate, or a potential client, that we may just not be on the same page. But whatever happens, make sure to do some introspection and really think about what you want. Because once you find your purpose, things seem to get a whole lot clearer from there.

STUFF WORTH REMEMBERING

The values that we chose for the company are what we use to guide us when we are lost—what we use as markers along the path when we have to make tough decisions or tools to motivate us to do better. They're something you live up to, but they're also bidirectional; both the employee and the employer should follow them.

Determining what values work for you and for a company is a pretty big deal. If you're doing just that, take your time and make sure you get it right the first time. And if you're a teammate, prospective or otherwise, see what kind of values the company has. They can help you decide whether you want to be there or not.

Values have purpose and create purpose.

Tips for Building a Values-Driven Culture

1. Define Values Collaboratively

   □ *Involve All Levels:* Don't just have executives pick values. Seek input from employees at all levels to identify shared beliefs.

   □ *Reflect Current Culture:* Look at existing cultural strengths, and build values around things already working well.

2. Leaders Must Model Values

   □ *Walk the Talk:* Leaders at all levels must consistently demonstrate the values in their words and actions. This sets the tone.

   □ *Call Out Incongruences:* When leaders see values not being followed, they must address it constructively. Hold each other accountable.

3. Reinforce and Reward

   □ *Call Out Examples:* Highlight examples of employees demonstrating the values. Recognize and praise these behaviors.

   □ *Incorporate into Reviews:* Make upholding the values a part of performance evaluations and promotion criteria.

4. Integrate into Operations

   □ *Hiring and Onboarding:* Screen for values alignment in hiring. Educate new hires on the values from day one.

   □ *Decision-Making:* Reference the values when making decisions. Will this align with our defined values?

- *Policies and Procedures:* Ensure company policies and procedures reflect the values.

5. Communicate Consistently

- *Talk about It:* Keep the values top of mind by discussing often in meetings, online, events, and so on.

- *Simple Messaging:* Distill the values into simple, repeatable statements and phrases. Avoid buzzwords.

CHAPTER THREE

GROWTH: IT'S GOT TO FEEL CHAOTIC

*If everything seems under control,
you're just not going fast enough.*

−MARIO ANDRETTI

In the late 1980s, right after Black Friday and the layoffs that followed, a man we'll call Mr. Z needed to find an option. He found it in a fledgling company nearby that made computer software. This was the '80s, after all, and while some people had a PC or Macintosh sitting in their home, they were nowhere near as common as they are today. Buying this kind of company was a risk and one he didn't want to take alone. And so, with the help of two of his friends, he purchased this small business and got to work.

It didn't take long for the two friends to bow out, but that was OK. Mr. Z worked hard every day to not only develop the software the company used but also help it to grow. He went from selling one product to three and then expanded further with paper products that worked with his software. Things were going well.

By the time things rolled around to the late 1990s, Mr. Z was at a very different point in his life professionally and personally. The last ten years were a rush with most of the work being performed by Mr. Z and his wife. It was too much though, so they decided to hire someone to help. Now the work was going even faster—almost too fast, one would argue—but Mr. Z kept his head above water and kept pushing forward.

The growth continued. Mr. Z's company dodged the dot-com boom and bust entirely and made it out not just unharmed but also flourishing. He now had three employees, which meant they could make more programs and more paper goods, and sell more overall.

The stress of the job was getting to him, however. This never-ending chaos was putting a strain on some of his relationships, making it difficult for him to not only succeed but also push forward.

It was then, in the middle of it all, that tragedy struck.

Mr. Z rented a small space within a larger building. It was one of those deals where you have a structure with five individual companies inside. His location consisted of four separate offices, a tiny warehouse, and two bathrooms. That last part was key, because in the midst of all this growth within the company, just after five o'clock on a Friday night, the feed line to one of the toilets would burst. It flooded the office, not only ruining the large PCs that sat on the floor but also wicking up the Sheetrock walls at least a foot. By the time a neighboring business tenant called him about it on Sunday, he knew he was in major trouble. He spent the day sweeping water out the warehouse door and trying to figure out how to salvage the situation. And crying. He did a lot of that, too.

This is where Mr. Z wanted to give up on his dream. He still wanted to grow as much as ever, but the almost glacial pace at which it was happening seemed to be more than he could handle. And now, with the destruction of his office, he had no idea what to do next. But as it turns out, the solution to both was the same: keep going and keep growing.

With growth as his intention, Mr. Z worked out a deal with the landlord. Not only would Mr. Z take over the office next door, but he would also pay for renovations to the space. Between his insurance coverage and his own building know-how, he could make the improvements he wanted without incurring too much debt. Now Mr. Z would double his footprint, have a completely redone office, and be able to bring on more employees.

That was exactly what he did. Soon the staff had doubled in size. Mr. Z picked up a huge new client that not only wanted the company's software but also needed them for consultation and guidance setting everything up. The office itself, although substantially bigger now, started to get pretty tight, but they made it work. Mr. Z had never been busier, and the business was prospering.

Because he focused on growth, Mr. Z finally realized the true potential in his business. He discovered the chaos of previous years wasn't his enemy but actually his motivator—a way to push himself forward even when he wasn't sure it would work. But it did work, again and again. Were there stumbles? Absolutely. But, just like he did after the flood, Mr. Z and his team always picked themselves up and pushed forward. The chaos itself was not only the motivator but also the driving engine of growth.

Mr. Z learned tremendous growth had to feel chaotic and occasionally uncomfortable. And when it did, the success that followed was tremendous.

The Basics of Growth

Now, if I were to tell you that growth was important here at RSi and for our business, you might respond with a resounding, "Yeah, no kidding." Fact of the matter is, every business wants to grow. It's only the exceedingly rare situation where you find a business that doesn't want to expand and sell more stuff. So yes, growth is an important thing here at RSi. But the reason why it's important, well, that's a whole other thing.

Let me explain through a quick and somewhat odd example of something a lot of people don't equate with growth: parking spaces.

A few years back, we ran into an issue with our desire to "Make Big," as we like to say. We wanted to expand—growth was a huge motivator for everyone on the team—but we were starting to run into a space issue. We simply didn't have enough room for the number of teammates we needed.

A little more clarity on the situation: Let's say that I've got a building with one hundred employees. It's doing well. We're making sales, and all is good. But we want to expand because our current office has exceeded its max capacity. We find a building, and it's perfect—all the square footage to house one thousand people, the highest speed connections everywhere. It's the perfect call center. We'd have room to double our staff easily. So far so good—as far as desk space. As we'd find out, creating places to park bodies is easy. However, finding spots to park cars driven by those bodies is much more difficult.

Having one thousand people means we'd also need one thousand parking spaces. Good luck finding a building with that. Most office buildings are made up of offices and not cubicle farms. The number of spaces outside matches the number of offices inside—typically 3.5 spaces per 1,000 square feet. For us and our density, we need seven to eight parking spots per 1,000 square feet. The cubicles throw off the ratio in a significant way. It's not ideal.

As you probably could guess, in the call center business, this is a very real problem, and it's one we ran into headfirst. If you want to move forward, you have to find the building. It's hard to get enough space to handle the amount of people you want on staff within a city's limits, so you often have to go to the suburbs. Problem then is your employees may or may not live closer to that main city. And if they have to travel, they'll need either public transportation or a car. More complications and less reliability. Which brings us to that last point.

This was the issue we had back in 2017, and it bordered on the perplexing. We wanted nothing more than to grow, grow, grow, but we knew we had to pump the brakes. Space was a problem, and parking was an even bigger problem. Before we could grow, we had to wait. And that put a frustrating crimp in our style. After all, at this point we were flying high, and this challenge was keeping us grounded. We preached growth all day, every day, and sitting still just didn't fit the story we were telling and selling to clients and prospective teammates.

This is about the time we thought we were really stuck. We needed a lot more employees, which meant more space, which meant much bigger parking lots. We were figuring out we couldn't easily change our location, so we had to change our thinking. Growth, after all, was key.

Fast-forward to today, and you've got a really obvious and easy solution: remote work. To be clear, had you told us to just have some of our employees work from home, we would've said that you were nuts. Between the culture building, management challenges, security concerns, turnover rate, internet latency issues, and everything else, there was no way we would move to a remote system. We had to find another alternative, so in 2018, we took the "best available" option that was just outside of the city. It wasn't ideal, but it would be good enough and support our growth habit until we could find better.

Then 2020 hit, and, well, you probably know that whole story.

Rather, you know everyone else's story. For us, this opened our eyes to a new opportunity. If—and this was a big "if" to us back then—we could move our employees to a remote system, solve all the IT problems, and ensure they were just as productive, we might have solved the growth problem. This could be more than the answer we were waiting for. It could be an absolute game changer.

We moved forward and did it fast. In fact, we were ahead of the curve. When the president shut down the country for two weeks in the middle of March, we already had our people in place, at home, ready to go. It was a huge push by our IT team—just mammoth—but they figured it out. And, as a result, we grew and grew.

Today, we're able to bring on teammates from all over the world. Opening up our system to remote associates meant that we were no longer limited to locals. Instead, we could have a team working virtually on the West Coast, while others were doing the typical eight o'clock to five o'clock schedule on the East Coast. Heck, we could have people dotting the landscape of the country—beyond, even— and it was no big deal. It meant that we could grow and finally fulfill our commitment to ourselves.

For us, growth is such an important part of our values that we put it first on the list. But, like the other core values we will discuss (Growth, Candor, No BCD, Team over Individual, and No ROI, No Spend), we're talking about more than just growing the top-line value.

However, before we get into that, we do have to state the obvious: revenue growth is important—incredibly important. After all, if we're not bringing in more revenue for our clients and ourselves, then not only do we stop growing, but we also could start going the opposite direction. The reason, our "why," is arguably more important.

Increased revenue gives us more opportunities, and with that comes flexibility in all areas of your business. Money in the bank means we can weather a recession or expand as necessary. We're a stronger competitor because we have more solid financial footing. But, more than anything, it's exciting for everyone we serve.

You've probably worked at a company with goals. This place had standards that you seemingly wanted to hit, and if you did, they'd throw a pizza party or something similar. Maybe you were a salesperson at a car dealership where they rang a bell whenever a vehicle was sold—or you heard that sound when you picked up your own ride. That feeling of success is important for not only you but also your team. The right energy means everything.

For us, we like to celebrate often and on a large scale. In fact, we probably spend an inordinate amount of time and energy celebrating when we achieve our revenue goals. It's a huge part of our effort to turning the business into a game.

You've probably heard of "gamification" before, but if not, I'll give you a quick lesson. The idea is to take a boring task (like working at a desk all day) and then assign it values like you'd find in a game or something like it. Here's an example: Say you want to create more widgets at your widget factory, but, let's face it, building those widgets are b-o-r-i-n-g. One way you could motivate your team is to assign point values to every widget made by each employee, and then show those points on a board in the break room. Whenever they head to lunch, they'll see where they're at in the system. And if they're close to first, they might push a little bit harder those next few hours to climb to the top of the chart. When you incentivize them with a prize—$100 gift certificate, pizza party, whatever—and it's something they really want, they'll work harder to get it. That whole process of turning tasks into a game is what gamification is all about, and it's one of the ways we make growth more fun here at RSi.

At RSi, gamification strategies fit with our culture of growth and make the workplace much better. When done right, everyday chores like calling an insurance company to settle a claim or helping a patient schedule an appointment become more fun, interesting, and competitive. This helps keep teammates be not only interested and motivated, but also more productive—by a lot.

Gamification, as we do it, also encourages a culture of continuous improvement and learning by setting clear goals, giving instant feedback, and giving rewards for accomplishments. This fits perfectly with a growth mindset that puts a lot of emphasis on learning, development, and new ideas, which are all things we work hard to encourage.

Keeping Ahead of the Competition

RSi does not live in a vacuum. We're a part of the healthcare industry that has a lot of twists and turns, and there are multiple companies out there that would love to have what we have. Competition is fierce.

Growth is one of our key drivers in solving that problem. New technologies come to the fore every day, and when they do, we need to determine whether or not they should be a part of our workflow. If so, we get in. If not, we move on—but either way, we decide based on growth. If this particular solution will help us grow, then we do it.

There are other benefits as well. If new technology will help out our clients—even just one of them—then we will give it solid consideration. After all, if one client needs something, future ones might as well. In a competitive market where many companies offer similar services, growth is one of the ways in which we stand out. We are never simply trying to maintain in any area and for anyone we serve.

This emphasis on growth is also how we can make connections with new clients. Think about any potential company that we would work with. They have tons of options, so why would they choose RSi? Well if other companies seem to be content where they are, and we're pushing to grow further, then don't we stand apart?

Sure, keeping ahead of the competition is just one component of the motivation for growth, and we understand that. But it's a component all the same and one that we should be very aware of.

Teammates

Another factor with growth? Teammates. Specifically, how many of them we have. Now there are a couple of reasons why the volume of team growth is important, and part of that just comes down to perspective.

First off, a major objective of any business is to make a profit, and we only add teammates when the business requires it for new clients or expansion with current clients. Therefore, when we see our teammate count rise, we know profits are rising as well.

Next, the sheer number of employees we have in our organization is a major force multiplier. Think about it: the more people we have, the more likely we are to find winners. These superstars challenge others to do better and lift the entire team up, too.

It's a pretty universal thing. Have you ever hung out with losers before? No judgment here; I've certainly had some "mistakes" in my day. But what you'll find when you do hang out with people who aren't that motivated, engaged, or are generally negative folks is how you start to fall into the same behaviors. It's like you're sucked into this negativity whirlwind, destined to live the rest of your life in mediocrity. And that's very, very far away from growth.

But when you hang out with superstars? That's the good stuff right there. Those folks make you feel motivated. You want to be a part of the lead group, so you push harder to meet or exceed your own goals. It's like hanging with superstars gives you superpowers of your own. It's pretty cool that way and happens very predictably.

Another great part of having more teammates? More diversity. Look, not everyone was raised like me—in a small, southern town with a party line for a telephone—and frankly, that's probably a good thing. When you have a different background, whether it's your childhood, race, gender, or the physical area you grew up in, you think about things differently than others, and this perspective contributes to a wide range of ideas of solutions.

I've got this friend of mine who lives in India. He's a great dude, an extremely talented journalist. Both of his parents are Indian, and so, one would assume he's been in the country all of his life. Nope. He was born in Omaha and lived there up until relatively recently. If you were to talk to him about India, he'd have his opinions for sure, but he's got a different perspective from the locals because he lived in Nebraska for the majority of his life.

Same thing applies to everything in our world at RSi. Those different and diverse opinions matter. They make all of us better teammates. Someone raised like me might not consider certain scenarios that come up on a phone call, for example. It's why we try to hire a wide variety of different people from all walks of life. Their opinions, where they come from, how they see things, and their circumstances matter.

Quick example: Depending on our office location, some of our teammates commute to work while others prefer public transportation. When the folks who hop into their car to make the drive to work forget their lunch one day, they can simply take a ride to a local establishment, place an order, and lament their mistake as they eat.

Now what about my teammates who decide to use public transit or rideshare? If they head out in a rush and forget their lunch, they're limited to what's in the break room. If we've only got chips and soda, they won't have much to choose from, right? One of our teammates had that exact scenario and pitched the idea of having food on hand that was healthier. A lot healthier actually, so we did just that—but more of the story is coming in a future chapter.

Expanding the numbers of a team with diverse individuals brings an incredible range of experiences, skills, perspectives, and ideas to the table. This is critical for creativity and problem-solving. Here's our top five reasons it matters, but there are certainly dozens more:

1. Greater Creativity

    ▫ Different perspectives mean different ways of thinking about the same problems, which leads to more creative and innovative solutions. Diverse teams tend to come up with more unique ideas because they bring a wide variety of experiences and knowledge to the table.

2. Faster Problem-Solving

    ▫ Diverse teams can bring a wider range of solutions to problems. This is because they can draw from a broad array of experiences, which allows them to come up with solutions more quickly than a more homogenous team might be able to. They're also more likely to challenge one another, leading to better thought-out solutions.

3. Improved Employee Engagement

- Employees are just more engaged in their work when they feel that they're a part of a diverse and inclusive environment. They feel more valued and recognized for their unique contributions, and this sense of belonging can significantly improve job satisfaction, productivity, and commitment to the organization.

4. Better Decision-Making

- Diverse teams make better business decisions. It's pretty simple. The different perspectives within the team can help prevent the dreaded groupthink.

5. Increased Profitability and Growth

- Companies with diverse leadership often see better financial results. This is believed to be a result of the improved decision-making, creativity, and innovation that comes from diversity.

The Opportunity Promise

Growth brings new opportunities, and that's another thing that's just so important. Like every other business in the world, we're constantly trying to figure out how to better engage our crew. One of our tips—and one that many companies use—is the promise of a brighter future. For us, that means growing skills and abilities while ascending within the company.

The more people on hand that we have, the more we grow, the more leadership positions and promotions are available. Everyone is eligible for these promotions and their corresponding raises.

In the past we've seen a lot of eye rolls about the topic. "Sure," they think, "you're going to give out promotions. That's just what my last boss told me." Their background has taught them not to trust management and what, in their experience, has often been empty promises.

The solution? You've got to be incredibly consistent about delivering on this commitment. Consistent positive action is key to the opportunity promise. We sincerely believe we must maintain a ruthless consistency throughout the organization as we become larger and larger. As we like to preach, "Be who you say you are and do what you said you would do."

People who work for the company today should be first on the list for promotions. They know the system, after all. Plus, they know where to make improvements. That's not something you get from an outside hire, not all the time, anyways. It's why we look internally first, particularly at those who have paid their dues.

Now a lot of companies boast about this kind of stuff, but we live by these values. Want proof? Ninety percent of our supervisors were internal promotions, ten out of twelve managers were internally promoted, and eight out of ten directors and assistant directors previously held different positions within RSi. Even our executive levels reflect this strategy. Well over half of the company officers started out at lower-level slots.

An example to illustrate: in July 2011, we had a recent graduate, a typical twenty something, start at RSi. We'll call him Bob, because that's his name. Bright guy, but he knew nothing about our industry. Nothing at all. In fact, he was choosing between us and a commissioned sales job selling frozen foods. He started at RSi as a collector. He learned the ropes and was mentored by folks at different levels throughout the organization. Soon enough he was promoted to supervisor.

A natural leader, he applied the lessons he'd learned as a point guard and quarterback in high school to the team he was charged with leading. It wasn't long before he was elevated to an interim manager spot, which was another step in his growth trajectory. With more clients came more expansion. Bob was made a permanent manager, the only one in the company at the time. This was still just the start. As the organization continued to expand in size and capacity, Bob continued to expand his capability and responsibility. Soon manager, he became director and then VP, and today he serves as our senior VP of operations for the entire company. Quite a rapid ascension for someone who had never stepped foot in a call center before he started. That's what growth can mean to a teammate.

We're pretty proud of these statistics, for sure. And it's just another major growth factor that works well for us and our team.

Ideas and Ideation

Now we've all heard about the tech industry and how crazy unimaginable technologies are being discovered in Silicon Valley. One of their mottos that has bitten them in the backside before is a popular one: "Move fast, and break things," originally coined by Mark Zuckerberg at Meta neé Facebook.[3] The idea behind the catchy phrase is to put aside the concept of "perfect," as that can stymie growth. Instead, by continuously pushing the boundaries of what's possible, your company will move forward. Sure, there will be a few broken eggs along the way, but that resulting omelet is going to be delicious. Well, that's the theory, anyway.

---

3   Isobel Asher Hamilton, "Mark Zuckerberg's New Values for Meta Show He Still Hasn't Truly Let Go of 'Move Fast and Break Things,'" Business Insider, February 16, 2022, https://www.businessinsider.com/meta-mark-zuckerberg-new-values-move-fast-and-break-things-2022-2.

In our case, growth allows our employees to use the first part of that phrase—"move fast"—to come up with and execute new ideas. They know that management wants the company to grow, and there may be a few bumps along the way. That's totally fine with the higher-ups, so folks at RSi take risks and come up with creative solutions to their problems.

That "creative" part is key. The implication is that our employees can figure out something that's out of the norm because it might help us move forward. It also implies that we are open to those new ideas, which, factually, we are. As a result, our company culture revolves around pushing to do things better, faster, and more efficiently, which means we're always looking to drive innovation and continuous improvement in all areas, not just tech.

This is a self-perpetuating cycle, too. You do something to improve the system, and it gets better. Then someone else does something to improve the system further, and it gets even better. You see where I'm going here. Whether it's company culture, process innovation, or a better way to have a staff meeting, ideas matter and innovation matters.

At the end of it all, it's about giving our clients better and more efficient systems. As a result, they will be more loyal and happier, which is always one of our end goals.

Skills

When you hire someone to talk on the phone, you're hiring a certain type of person who has, in the words of the great business prophet, Liam Neeson's character in the movie *Taken*, "a very particular set of skills." Every new person who comes through the door can not only do their intended position but also has other abilities to be discovered along our journey together. Attributes that may not directly apply to their role here but could further on.

Quick story about a buddy of mine. He was in his thirties, recently married, and had a hard time getting into his chosen profession. Instead, he worked as an office manager, toiling away and restoring classic cars on the side. He always wanted to be a writer, but he had to do it when he wasn't working his day gig. He was married, after all, and had a family to support.

An opportunity popped up for him at a local publication, but it was a fashion magazine. This guy wore Dickies and T-shirts with a Chevy bowtie on them, and clearly his interests were not in lifestyle and clothing stories. But he applied anyway, and, after a few rounds of interviews, he got the job.

But why? Was it his skill set? Maybe, but years later he would ask his boss from back then what it was that made him stand out. It turns out the manager wanted another type of voice on the team. Someone who wasn't embedded in the fashion world, but an outsider who had a different perspective. Specifically, a male perspective, since the readership skewed female, and they wanted to balance it out a bit. Did he get the job because of his abilities? Yes, but, as he would find out later, that wouldn't be enough. The job he initially applied for actually went to someone else. But because he had this different perspective, that boss opened up a new role just for him. Not because he was that good at the role, but because he wasn't like everyone else. The fact that he was different was his asset.

We interview people all the time, and we're constantly looking for those kinds of qualities. When people have something unique to offer, it opens up new opportunities for the company and allows us to attract more and better clients while we expand into different areas.

We are lucky to be in a position where we can value character and attitude as much as we do skills, and it's pretty cool.

Capacity

The thing about experience is it takes time. Just think about your own childhood. Did you know how to open a can or use the microwave when you were five? Probably not, but by the time you hit sixteen, you could do both pretty easily. So with that said, we've accepted reality: growing our experience level does take time. But it shouldn't take thirty years, though.

We have a pretty straightforward mentality about the process. Basically, we believe the more we do, the quicker we'll gain experience. That means failing fast and often, which we do every day. This isn't a new concept. As we said earlier in this chapter, "Move fast, and break things." It was a mantra for years at Facebook, and it's something many others have done as well, including us. It leads us to try new things, all with growth in mind.

No matter the idea, if it seems to have any merit at all, we make every possible effort to prototype it and give it a shot. Some call it a version of design thinking, which is a solution-based approach to solving problems.[4] We simply say, "Let's try it, and see how it works." Maybe it should be called the southern version of design thinking?

We believe in the teammates here at RSi and love this methodology. Would it inspire you? Is it the type of thing that would motivate you to try new things? For most of our staff, it does that and more. It's why we continue to chart "experience" as one of our key growth factors.

---

4   "Design Thinking," Interaction Design Foundation, accessed September 25, 2023, www.interaction-design.org/literature/topics/design-thinking#:~:text=Design%20 thinking%20is%20a%20methodology,ways%2C%20create%20numerous%20 ideas%20in.

Impact and Reach

Now "impact" has a lot of different meanings. For us, we're not thinking about the impact on our company as a whole but instead the individual people who make up the community.

The idea here is the larger we are, the more lives we can touch. Those are the lives of our teammates, the client's employees, and the folks in the communities we work in.

Why would any of that matter? After all, if you want to take a cold and callused look at the business world, your goals are about revenue, not anything to do with the community, right?

We look at the bigger picture. For us, if we give back to the community, whether it's through jobs or other methods, they will support us as well. It's a reciprocal relationship, and we appreciate that.

Reach is a similar situation. Geographic growth is important for a multitude of reasons. Name recognition, for one, is pretty critical. If RSi becomes known as the place to go to for an RCM provider, then that helps us bring in more clients, then more employees, and, of course, grow.

But that same reach also brings in more volume, capability, and variety of talent to the company. Let's go back to the 2020 COVID-19 scenario. We had to be creative to get people working for us quickly, from home, without any IT problems. We also soon realized we didn't have to look for teammates just in South Carolina. We could go anywhere. Again, geographic reach. That adds to the diversity of our people and our experience, which gives us the enjoyment of having broader influence, too. It all circles back.

Keeping a Good Thing Going

Nobody wants the party to end. While work isn't always fun, we like it to be whenever possible. And if we want to protect our future, a.k.a.

keep a good thing going, we need to prove to our stakeholders we're such a good investment, and we should be able to do what we want to do moving forward. Consider it a blank check of sorts, in that we're allowed to make the right decisions—as much autonomy as you can get in these kinds of scenarios, anyway. And that's important.

Remember Michael Jordan? Of course, you do. That man knew not only the power of a good team but also what kind of sway he held over the group. He had more influence on the bench than whoever his coach was at the time, and we want to be the same way. By continuing to grow, we can help ensure that happens.

This also helps with our employees. As we grow, so do they. We offer all sorts of options for career development and training, so if they want to step up their skill set and advance, we're here for them. They're happier because they know we care enough to invest in their future, and we're happier because we have happy employees. There's a whole lot of happy in there.

One other thing to note? The economies of scale associated with growth. Fact is, the bigger we get, the lower the cost of the services we provide. We can be more profitable and then pass savings on to our clients, and everyone is—again with this word—happy.

Survival

And then, the important one. Now all of these things are important, obviously. That said, survival is pretty key to the whole equation. So with that in mind, let's put this into context via example.

If you're an animal, what kind of animal would you want to be? Would you rather become a field mouse or a whale? An elephant or an insect? Thing is, when you're a tiny animal, you've got some advantages. For one, you can be more nimble, make fast moves when necessary, and maneuver in and out of all sorts of situations. But the big animal? They're harder to take down. An elephant can succumb to attack, but it takes a lot of lions to do the job, whereas a bird can take out a field mouse in a hurry.

Now we don't want to compare ourselves to anyone in the animal kingdom, but the fact remains that it's easier to survive cataclysmic changes if you're a bigger company than it is if you're smaller. While we know that we're not Apple, Meta, Ford, or any of those companies, we do occupy a space in our industry of about four thousand other organizations. We're in the top fifty in size and revenue, and that gives us a much better chance of surviving the next round in a competitive selection process than it would if we were in the bottom fifty. Big is better than little in nearly all things but certainly in our business—especially as it relates to stability and survival.

October 2019 to March 2020

Let me close out this chapter with a quick little story.

Back in October 2019, we picked up a new investor and, with it, huge expectations. We were being called upon to do big things, and we were very excited about the opportunities that lay ahead of us. We'd have lots of resources to work with, too. It meant everyone in the company felt like we were really rolling. Good days were ahead of us.

December? A record month. January? Same thing. February? You know it. Everything we've planned out is working, and, more importantly, everyone is having a blast. It was working out just like we planned.

Then, well, like I said earlier in this chapter, you know what happened next. Except this time, let's go into the specifics.

When COVID-19 hit, the alarm bells sounded everywhere. Some companies decided to lay off employees, while others shut down entirely. It seemed like every strategy to reduce the size and scope of our operation was on the table. But not for us.

We saw that road ahead of us and decided we, the senior leadership, should figure out a path forward. We looked at our core values, and it didn't take long to see the first one on the list applied in this face of the situation we were facing: growth. We couldn't quit. No way. We would find that path and use growth as our guide.

A plan was made. We're primarily a BPO (business process outsourcer, for those keeping score)/call center organization, and although we had not considered moving to remote work previously, now we saw it as our only path forward. And that's exactly what we did. Everyone on the team moved to a remote role, and we announced that our absolute intention was twofold:

1. Keep everyone working. No cuts, no layoffs. No reductions in pay.

2. Keep everyone safe and healthy.

To make all that happen, we instituted daily huddles with all our teams to make sure they understood our commitment to them, our clients, the organization, our investors, and our growth goals. We wanted the whole team to be on the same page so that there could be no questions about how dedicated we were to keep everyone not only working and safe but somehow still grow in the process, as well.

Engagement was also an issue. We couldn't ring any bells or have pizza parties anymore, so we had to figure out options to keep people involved. We did just that and celebrated our wins even louder and more often than we did previously. We just did everything virtually. And often.

Oh, and we also made sure everyone knew that we were not adjusting goals, targets, or expectations in any way. We would not only push through this hard time, but we would also survive and thrive.

The year 2020 was our best year ever. We increased revenue 22 percent compared to 2019, and we hired an additional 112 teammates. The year 2021 was even better, thanks to the incredible efforts building out a remote strategy we implemented in 2020. Our company gained an extra 52 percent increase in revenue and another 126 teammates. Over the course of the first twenty-four months of the pandemic, while other companies were stalling, we literally doubled both revenues and team size.

So yes, growth is important here at RSi. Our growth mindset not only pushed us through one of the most difficult times in world history but also brought us to bigger and better things. It sounds crazy, but it worked.

STUFF WORTH REMEMBERING

With growth, there comes a measure of chaos. We want to get that up front, and we use that specific word for a reason.

If you're fully committed to growth, you don't always wait for the planets to align. You don't always dot the "i" and cross the "t." When a client has a need and you know you have the ability to help alleviate their pain, we dive in and go at it double time. Yes, it's chaotic, and it's our choice. Because at the end of the day, we believe if we always wait for perfect, we will never get started.

Tips for Fostering a Culture of Growth

1. Leadership Focus on Growth

   - *Vision:* Senior leaders must establish and communicate a clear vision focused on growth. This provides alignment and motivation.

   - *Role Modeling:* Leaders at all levels should role model a growth mindset in their own development. This shows others that growth is valued and supported.

2. Empower Innovation

   - *Idea Sharing:* Create open channels where all employees can share new ideas and innovations. Act upon the best suggestions.

   - *Fail Fast Environment:* Allow people to take risks and fail fast without repercussion. This encourages creativity.

3. Reward Growth Behaviors

   - *Development Goals:* Incorporate growth and development goals into performance management. Recognize those who expand their skills.

   - *Celebrate Wins:* Publicly celebrate growth milestones and wins. This reinforces the value of growth.

4. Hire for Growth Potential

   - *Screen for Growth Mindset:* Assess candidates not just on current skills but also on their potential to grow and develop new capabilities over time.

   - *Diversity of Perspectives:* Seek diversity in backgrounds and perspectives to maximize creativity and innovation.

5. Continuous Learning Culture

- *Training Programs:* Offer internal training programs and access to external development resources. Remove barriers to learning.

- *Knowledge Sharing:* Facilitate mentorships, job rotations, and knowledge sharing across the organization. Maximize learning from experience.

CHAPTER FOUR

CANDOR

. . . .

There is no diplomacy like candor.

—E. V. LUCAS

L et me tell you a little story about a man we'll call Charles. He led a rather standard life, but he had an unusual method of making friends.

See, as a child, Charles learned early on that sometimes it was hard to get other kids to like him. So he did what a lot of people do in that situation: he lied.

At first, it was a simple one. Maybe he told a friend that his father, a manager at a local business, was actually the owner of the said company. Then it was an uncle who was wealthy and mysterious. It wasn't that Charles wanted to do harm to other people, far from it. No, he just desired contact with the outside world so much that he felt he had to shape himself to meet the moment. Nothing major, right?

There were no repercussions for his actions. Once, in the fourth grade, Charles stayed up all night to create a beautiful-looking book report that was filled with borderline nonsensical language. Anyone who paid even a small amount of attention would realize he hadn't read the book, so the report itself was gibberish. But it looked good. Guess what? He got an A+, and his work was paraded in front of the classroom as an example of what good was. See, Charles now learned that his lying wasn't a bad thing and could actually be rewarded. And now he was even cognizant of what he was doing.

I'm not afraid of using bad language here and there, but I'm going to respect the idea that you may not be, reader. With that in mind, let's just call Charles a level one "BSer."

Now a struggling kid in his early twenties, Charles stumbled from job to job, but somewhere along the way, he realized he was good at making furniture. So, he started a carpentry business out of his garage at home. Eventually, he had to move that business into a sublet space nearby, and then again to another space, but this one all his own in a local industrial complex. He brought on a business partner, even though nothing was very well formalized with his company, and he felt like things were good. He wasn't always honest with his new partner, but frankly, he had never been honest with anyone, so that was nothing new. But then the dining room table happened.

Charles was commissioned to build a custom dining room table for a client. It was big—about eight feet long—with six matching chairs, upholstered in white fabric. The concept would produce a beautiful result, and even though Charles had never created anything like it before, he had confidence in his skills and pressed forward. The customer paid in full, and he got started.

Unsurprisingly, as it turned out, our man Charles was a little bit overconfident. He promised the table in a month, and when one month turned into six, the customer got very irritated. Things started to stack up against Charles. First, some of the lumber was stolen from his shop. He was cash strapped as it was, so getting replacement wood was going to take some time. Then the upholstery became more complex than he wanted, and, ultimately, Charles became—how can we say it?—lazy. It was fun being in his mid-twenties with his own business. He didn't have much for expenses other than rent, so why stress? Why not go out and party with his girlfriend and hit the bars regularly? The work would still be there, right?

Things came to a head one morning in the spring. It had been almost a year now since the table was ordered, and the customer came for a surprise visit. There was the table, sitting under what seemed like an inch of dust, untouched for at least a month. The customer was livid—understandably so—and started yelling. They were so loud, in fact, that other people in the industrial complex started coming outside to see what the fuss was all about. It got bad. Real bad. And that was when not only the customer got mad but so did the partner as well. It was a horrible day for Charles. Things seemed to be unraveling.

Later that night, the partner came to Charles and said they wanted to end the relationship. Charles agreed and gave the entire business over to his now former partner, including most of the tools in the shop. There was no money trading hands or anything; it was just a man who realized how far he had fallen and giving it all up.

There's no happy ending to this parable; Charles lost everything that day. His business, his partner, and most of his friends who also knew what happened were all tired of putting up with his BS. "Enough is enough," they would say, and then walk away from him and his questionable ways.

He needed a job, so he took one delivering pizzas. This gave him lots of time while driving to think about what he had done and debate the choices he made up to this point. It was a hard time. He had no one to talk to other than his dog. As a result, he sunk deeper and deeper into a pit of depression.

It was then that he was handed a lifeline—a way out of delivering pizzas and instead doing new things. Someone who knew Charles only peripherally provided him with an opportunity to reinvent himself, even though they didn't know that was the case at the moment. As it turns out, Charles dabbled in photography here and there, and he started to get some attention for his work online. A person reached out who wanted to use his services, and he could start anew as a photographer.

It was then Charles had his epiphany. He couldn't keep things going the way they were. His constant looseness with the truth had torn his life apart, and he needed to make a very serious change, because if he kept lying his way through life, it would crash down around him again.

No more lying. No more BSing his way through events and making things up. Instead, he would tell the truth, almost to a fault. Forget the tiny white lies, even if it would make someone feel better. Nope, it was telling the truth or nothing else.

From that point on, Charles was as honest as possible. He never lied, not even a little bit, and his business flourished. Soon he was taking photographs for popular websites, and that led to not only a successful business of his own but also the ability to create a team of photographers and his own little studio. It was everything he wanted, and it was all because Charles chose candor.

What Is Candor?

We can get into the dictionary definition if you like, but we all have smartphones and we could look it up ourselves, right? So let's go with what we at RSi consider to be candor: frank, open, honest, straightforward, truthful, sincere, unvarnished, and forthright. These are all ways to describe candor from an RSi perspective.

But if we're getting down to brass tacks, candor, to us, means having the tough or uncomfortable conversations as a matter of practice. These are the ones nobody really wants to have, and most often both participants are squirming a little. It's mid-2000s comedy levels of awkward, you know?

Let's put this into context with another quick story.

The Case of the Controlling Client

A few years back we took on a private equity partner. There's a lot of courtship involved in that whole process, which, in our case, took about six months. And, as is natural in these types of things, they checked in regularly to see how the business was growing and how things were materializing.

Around this time, we discovered that one of our current clients wanted to expand the operation. This would've been the most comprehensive contract we had and the largest. They wanted to go big and were very excited, as were we. This was huge for us and the company, so we shared the information with our prospective investor, and they got excited, too. There was massive potential, and it got to the point that we're discussing the project daily. The investors got even happier, and everyone was ecstatic. It was a good time.

Except, as it turns out, for our employees.

We learned that this big prospective contract and the Hospital System attached to it had a bit of a values mismatch with us. It's not that we don't want to work hard, and it's not that we don't want to do the right thing. But this particular client treated us and our people poorly. And that wasn't going to fly.

We talk a lot here about how we, the company, want to be your, the customer's, best employee. We want to partner with you to enable your goals, right? Well, this client certainly didn't treat us like a partner, and we certainly weren't treated like any employee that I've ever had.

But the money, right? Yes, the money. So we trudged forward, doing our best to keep a good face and all that. I was at the front of the line, taking the brunt of the abuse. Now it was my decision to do that, but still, it wasn't fun to deal with. That said, this wasn't my team's decision at all. They didn't want this drama, but they followed my lead and took a beating with the client.

Now this is where things get a little funky. Everyone on the team wanted to impress this client and do a good job overall. They knew that I had a lot on my plate and, as a result, didn't come to me with issues. Instead, they worked to resolve them internally, which meant we were cycling through leaders—and therefore connections with the client—regularly, and that client didn't like any of them.

That's not to say that we were firing people, because that certainly wasn't the case. Instead, we'd move them over to different teams, switch out a project manager or two—even executive leadership—and keep pushing forward. My judgment was clouded by the big dollar signs involved, and attached to that was how our investor felt about the project.

Eventually, things hit a breaking point. Bob, our VP of operations, the aforementioned former janitor from the introduction, comes up and says, "Brent, this doesn't comport with what you preach."

He continued, explaining how our core values fit into this scenario. Then he says, "I'm going to practice candor here and tell you that we all want to quit this deal. Nobody wants to be involved in it. They don't respect this. They don't appreciate what we're doing, and no matter what we do, the client always finds a reason to be mad at us."

I took what he said and thought about it, but things still didn't quite stick. But Bob just broke the seal on this whole deal. Once he complained, so did ten, twenty, and then what seemed like fifty more people. They all came to me saying the same thing. If they were even remotely connected to the project, they complained. Frontline employees practiced candor with me and said, in plain English, "I just don't want to do this anymore." At some point, even thick-headed guys like myself have to pick up what other people are putting down. It was time to terminate this relationship.

This doesn't happen a lot in our industry. Companies don't want to come across as being too difficult to work with, which would make it tough for them to pull in future clients. We've never shied away from it and have terminated those relationships multiple times. But this time felt a lot different. It was on a huge scale, and had a high degree of visibility with our potential investor. We brought in ownership, the executive team—seemingly everyone was involved.

Then we brought it to the client and explained our terms. Yes, it was a lucrative contract, but when we evaluate the concern we have for our teammates and the respect we have for ourselves, it obviously wasn't mutual, so we had to pull the plug on the deal. And once we did, it was amazing how things took off from there.

What I didn't realize before was what a mental and emotional drag this client had been on the company. Team members started to look at us a little bit differently. After all, here we were talking a big game about respect and all that, but that client didn't follow our rules. Would we—management—take the big check and step on the company's values? By terminating this deal, we showed that we wouldn't.

But what about the investor? Would they stick with us or bail because we chose our values over profit? Well, they ultimately did make the investment in RSi. They told us that they were going to let us run our business. They didn't want to manage the organization for us; for them, this was no different from buying stocks.

Obviously it all worked out in the end, as we're here today still kicking butt and taking names. But that isn't always a foregone conclusion. Situations like this happen all the time, and if it wasn't for our values, we wouldn't be where we are today. We work hard to foster an environment where everyone can speak their mind and express their feelings fully. It's a challenge for new folks to get used to for sure, but once they figure it out, it doesn't take long for them to see everyone at every level practicing candor.

Management and Everyone Else

Let's take a moment to talk about the weird class breakdown that seems to happen in a company, no matter its size. At a very rudimentary level, you have employees and management. Both work for the company, and both collect a paycheck. But the differences here are in how each is perceived by others both in and outside of the organization.

Do you remember when you were in high school and there were all these different cliques of people floating around? There were the jocks, the popular kids, the honor students—groups like that. Management and their employees tend to form similar classes. When you're in management, at least in the beginning, you might not recognize the plights your employees are going through because you're on a different level. And as an employee, management is intimidating. You don't want to go to them for anything if you don't have to, and sometimes just talking to them can cause you to break out into a sweat.

That's not how things work here at RSi, and one of the reasons is candor. There's no meeting behind the meeting where management secretly talks about who they're firing next. Everything's open and on the table, so you always know where you stand. For better or worse, but there is no guessing.

This isn't posturing or platitude, either. Sometimes we'll hire teammates for a particular position contingent on whether or not a new client will sign on, and we tell them exactly that. If the client doesn't sign, you will still have a position, but it may be in a different area. Other times employees worry that we'll lose a client, and, should they talk to management, we'll tell them where we stand with that client and what is next for them. Again, for better or worse, they will know everything we know.

This, for both sides of the table, is a liberating experience, and if you haven't experienced it at your company, well, you need to think about exercising some candor. Because really, this has happened to all of us. We didn't wake up one day and enter higher management; I spent my time in the trenches, too. I know what it's like to ask the bosses whether or not I'll have a job tomorrow and then watch them lie to my face. It's terrifying to be in that situation, and I certainly don't want anyone else to be in that place with me. It's why candor, and its use here at RSi, is such a big deal.

Now there is a problem with all this, particularly if you're new to this kind of structure. The first feeling new teammates get is suspicion. What is this company hiding from me? That's a natural response and something we talk about a lot. We do weekly meetings and monthly staff meetings, and some are about general subjects. We always hit the core five values, including candor, which helps show people that we believe and act on what we say. It's kind of codified and memorialized that we do actually live these values, and we hope our employees see that. Of course, we know it only matters in practice.

Usually it takes three to six months for people to believe it. Say one of them falters in the job, and they're concerned that they're not hitting their standards. Are they going to be OK? Yeah, for sure. We want to see progress, not perfection, and we want this progress to continue as for all of our time together. And as long as that's happening, they'll be fine. But like I said, it takes some time usually for employees to figure out we're "practicing what we preach" when we say that we believe in candor.

Now this works both ways, obviously. One great example of this is when we hire for a new role. The very first thing we do is put the job posting out internally and let all of our employees know what we're looking for. Anyone can apply for any role, whether it levels up or levels down. It gives everyone an opportunity to try something new or get a raise. Remember, this is part of our commitment to growth internally.

But the thing is, sometimes we have to practice candor in those scenarios, too. If the employee doesn't have the specific skills or their past results don't match what the role requires for the company to accomplish its goals, well we're going to have to tell them the truth: we don't have any evidence that they're going to be able to pull it off. It's respectful, thoughtful, direct, and nearly always appreciated.

Trust, Don't Hate

Candor can be interpreted as being frank, but sometimes, if we're not careful, it can be laced with derision. "Well, I was just being honest," can be absolutely accurate, but it doesn't mean you have to be judgmental or a jerk. What you need to do instead is lean more on the trust that's been built.

So let's put this back into that employee promotion scenario from before. If I'm practicing candor, I can speak openly and honestly about the situation. I can tailor the way I speak to the employee based on their current role within the company, and I can also be very straightforward. But there's also no reason to be unkind, hypercritical, or rude.

This is part of the issue with candor, particularly with people new to the concept. If they're not careful, they can turn honesty into a weapon, making a judgment of the other people in the process. It's passive-aggressive in the worst way and turns the concept of candor on its head. We guard against this at every turn.

Instead, what candor—when properly applied—should do is actually create trust within your organization. It's a no BS business, which means whenever someone tells you something, they're saying the truth. They trust you to cover them when there's a problem, and you can trust them to do the same.

All that said, we're not perfect. There have been moments where people falter with practicing candor. We're only human, after all. But it's always the goal, and it's also substantially better than what you might find at other organizations. In fact, you've probably seen your share of backstabbing, ladder-climbing, and other corporate shenanigans that nobody likes in the end.

And that's what makes candor such a big deal, particularly when it's done correctly. If the person isn't mean or passive-aggressive, and you know they're telling you the truth, it's absolutely liberating. And once you've experienced it in the workplace, you'll never want to go back.

The Start-Up CEO

Let's put all this into practice for a moment.

A while back, there was this small start-up running in the technology area in Houston. Their CEO, who we'll call Ms. Felicia, has done what a founder does: poured all of her time, money, and energy into developing their product, and she convinced herself that it will be a huge success.

Finally, after months of work, Ms. Felicia pushed the product out into the market, and the market responded with a big, fat nothingburger. Initial sales were super slow, and the people who did buy the product were not happy with it. Ms. Felicia, as one could expect, was despondent. What could've gone wrong? Everything was perfect, right? But as it turns out, it wasn't.

Ms. Felicia loved and believed in this product so strongly that she couldn't see the forest for the trees. The product was flawed; she just couldn't see it.

Flash forward a few months, and a potential investor comes into the office to hear Ms. Felicia pitch the product. At this point, she had done all but throw in the towel on this thing and wasn't really even sure why he's taking the meeting. But she decided to meet with him anyway, and beforehand she decided to take a different approach. Instead of expounding on the virtues of her formerly favorite product, she chose to instead be candid about its weaknesses.

As she laid out his case for the product, she also took time to address sales. Ms. Felicia explained how the product isn't performing as well as she had hoped, but her team was working hard to figure it all out and address the issues. Oh, and by the way, would the investor have any advice for how to improve the product?

A lot of investors would've walked out of the office, ticked off by Ms. Felicia's failures. But instead, the investor was impressed by her transparency and honesty. In fact, he saw potential in the company and ultimately decided to invest. Now with the two of them working together, the organization was able to make significant improvements to the product, and it became a huge success.

The takeaways? Because she was upfront with this investor about her product's flaws and was candid about its downfalls, she realized that being transparent and honest in your business is not a weakness but a huge strength. It can help build lasting relationships and drive success, too. As a result, Ms. Felicia made a commitment to always being truthful and candid in her dealings with others, and her business thrived as a result.

Transparency and Honesty

Another key benefit of candor? Transparency.

It's easy enough to start at a job and feel like people are hiding something. I've got a friend of mine who once told me about how he went to get a job at this major corporation, and he was excited once he was offered the job. The day he started though, everyone seemed to be walking on eggshells. He didn't know how divisive the boss was or how the company was actually owned by a venture capital firm that was actively trying to shut it down, so they could cut losses and reallocate their investment elsewhere. Had there been a little bit more transparency in the interview process, he might have looked at the role differently and been more prepared once he started. But they didn't, so he didn't. And it all became a big mess.

People don't often practice transparency because they're worried about the results. Take my buddy's scenario. The company probably thought that if they told him all about the problems at the place, he'd run away and not want to work there. But some people—my friend included—love those kinds of challenges. He would have been more excited to start the job and could have excelled. But again, because they weren't transparent, he came in unprepared and more than a little bit scared about his future.

Point is, if we're not forthright with people, their imaginations will absolutely fill in all gaps, and the results are rarely positive. Shoot people straight, and let them make their own decisions with all the information and live with the fact that not everyone will jump on board.

This all comes back to making decisions. It's hard to make a tough call when you don't have all the information. Transparency gets you that right out of the gate, which allows the decision-making process to run smoother. That increases speed, which means we get more done quicker than usual.

Remember those backstabbing, ladder-climbing, horrible corporate people we talked about earlier who will do anything to get ahead? Transparency helps a ton there, too. If I know what you know, and we're all on the same page, it's pretty hard not to see some of those things coming.

Think about it from the other side, too. When a client walks into the office or talks to someone on the phone, they may even expect the other person to be a little bit deceitful. I mean, we all have that concept in our head of the horrible high-pressure salesperson who got you to buy that trashy car you bought when you were twenty. Salespeople have a bad reputation because of it, and so most people go into a sales situation assuming that they're going to hear exaggerations.

It makes sales tougher for everyone, sure, which is why transparency helps so much. Once people understand that we're not lying to them regularly, you can almost see their faces relax. It's awesome.

This also means that people who do buy RSi's services are more loyal when they experience our level of candor. Even if we make a mistake along the way, people still appreciate what we do and how we respond. And that's because we'll admit what happened, be fully transparent about the whole situation, and resolve it as best as possible. This goes a long way with our clients.

But most important, transparency gets you honesty. Look, this is hard for everyone to accomplish, but when you truly speak honestly and openly with clients and your teammates, you get all of the benefits. Problems get solved faster. Decisions are made more quickly, and you feel better about what you're doing. When you know someone is talking straight to you, don't you feel better about them and what they're saying?

There are a lot of organizations that don't practice this, where animosity is part and parcel of the job, and almost considered a feature and not a bug. We don't want that here, so we don't practice it. And frankly, even if you don't ever want to work with us, that's fine. As we like to say, "We are not a fit for everyone," but candor is still an important rule to follow in your life.

The Yellow Sheet of Paper

Back in the mid-1990s, there was a kid who was just turning eighteen. His parents had bought him his first car, a 1988 Daihatsu Charade, with a three-cylinder motor and a five-speed transmission. The Daihatsu was, as you could probably expect, absolute garbage. So much so that just two years later and thousands of dollars in repair bills, it was time to trade it in for something new.

The kid had some money put away from his job at Target, but this time his parents were going to help him out. They would buy the car for cash, and he would make payments to them—$200 a month. He could make it happen, so he started looking.

He wanted a truck—a Toyota standard-cab mini truck, specifically—and he dug through the local newspapers to find a sale. And find one he did, with two separate dealerships offering the same deal: $9,999 plus adds for the truck, with "adds" being "additional items" like air conditioning and the like. The kid wanted two adds, the aforementioned a/c as well as carpet, which wasn't going to raise the price high enough to affect much. Now he just had to work out the specifics with his dad.

The dad sat down with the kid, and they worked out how it was going to go down. They would go to the dealership and try to work some numbers. Chances were pretty good that the deal wasn't going to happen because of the trade, but hey, they'd give it a shot. The key, the dad noted, was to always be honest, show respect, and be ready to leave at any time.

The pair drove down to the dealership in the Daihatsu, found a truck, and started haggling with the salesperson. This lasted for an hour or so, with the leasing manager coming out (they weren't leasing the car), and then the financing manager coming out (they weren't financing it), until it came time to talk about the trade-in.

"Well," the salesperson told the dad, "we think we can offer you $500 for the Daihatsu, and that's the best we can do."

The kid put his hands on the armrests of the chair to lift himself up, but the dad put out his hand to stop the son's ascent. That's when the father pulled a folded sheet of yellow paper out of his pocket. He then unfolded it once, then again, and again, and one last time until it was completely open. The dad turned the piece of paper around so the salesperson could read it and slide it onto the desk in front of them.

"Kelley Blue Book values the car at $2,500. Let's get a little bit closer to that, and then we'll talk."

Another hour goes by, and the salesperson is pulling out all the tricks. He's trying hard to get the father and son to bite on a different truck, different deal, more options—anything to change what was obviously a sale they advertised to bring people in to upsell them. But the duo wasn't biting, and that's when the salesperson threw in the towel.

"I'm sorry," he said, "I don't think we can work anything out."

The dad and son raised up out of their chairs, and the older one said, "That's fine. Thank you for your time," and shook the salesperson's hand.

As soon as they were about twenty yards away from the now-shut showroom door, the son turns to his father and says, "So are we off to the other dealership now?"

And the dad, without skipping a beat or even looking toward his child says, "Nope. They're going to come out and get us."

The kid was perplexed, but he headed toward the Daihatsu anyways. Just as his hand hit the door handle, the doors to the showroom flew open. "Excuse me, sir! I think we have a deal!"

And about an hour later, the son was driving home his brand-new truck.

On the drive home, he thought about what would become a milestone in his life. His dad could have lied about the condition of the Daihatsu or tried to lowball them on the truck. And he could have harassed their sales team, abusing them to get the deal done. But instead, he stayed calm, collected, and, most of all, honest about his expectations coming into the deal and what he wanted out of it. There was no posturing, no loud noises, and no misrepresented truths.

Things could have gone a lot differently that day, and they didn't. In the end, the good guys won out because of kind, respectful candor.

Disagreements

Ever get into a fight with your significant other? It's not always a great experience, and it can be quite frustrating for everyone involved, particularly if one or both people are hiding something. Now imagine what would change if people were honest and candid instead.

The ability to prevent misunderstandings and confrontations is key to what we do at RSi. When a stakeholder comes to the table with a problem, we can guarantee that everyone involved is aligned and on the same page because we communicate with one another in a straightforward manner. There's no hiding behind corporate language or deception from other employees. It's all out in the open.

Because of that, we don't have as many disagreements and conflicts, and the ones we have don't last long. Frankly, these disagreements can be very costly in ways that are not immediately obvious. Think about all of the hours wasted on confrontations at your last job. That argument between the manager and his employee—what did that cost in lost time, and how much did that sour the relationship? Did they lose an employee in the process? That means someone else needs to get hired, which involves HR doing a lot of work, and then there's the hours of training. By the time you're done, one conflict over something trivial can turn into tens of thousands of dollars. But if everyone was up front and honest, you would invest only the actual amount of time necessary to identify, discuss, and resolve the issue.

Then there's the hit to the reputation. If we're seen as having infighting, messy employees, who's going to want to work with us? As a potential client, you don't want us as your vendor. And that's just externally. What about internally? Well, we can guarantee to our customers that all of our expectations are aligned on both sides of the fence, because we communicate with all of the stakeholders in an open and straightforward manner. It lessens the likelihood of conflicts, which can cost a ton of money and time, plus the aforementioned hit to our reputation.

Now obviously we can't guarantee everything. There will be misunderstandings here and there—that's just part of the world we live in. But because we practice candor and transparency, we know the chances of that happening are low. Combine that with our culture of respect and understanding, and you get a scenario where everything is more harmonious, whether you're on our team or you're a client.

How to Start Practicing Candor

Here at RSi, we didn't just jump into the candor pool with both feet. Although it existed in some areas, spreading it to everyone was key, but it wasn't easy. However, the benefits far outweighed the alternative, so we stuck with it and are better for it today.

But what about you and your team or organization? Or just you as an individual? How do you start practicing more candor?

You're going to get a healthy amount of skepticism by your peers, and that's to be expected. Who can be honest all the time? That's why you have to start with yourself. Be the example that they can follow and—this is the important part—ask them to give you feedback.

Can you take it as well as you dish it out? That's the question they're going to answer on their own. And your job here is to be honest and, well, candid. You want to provide whatever straightforward answer you can so they'll know you're legit in both your attitude and your practice. Is it going to be easy? No, not really. But it's a good step forward in building that trust.

This same concept moves forward when teammates have their one-on-ones with their managers on all levels. If each party is candid with the other, then there's no shuffling around awkward issues. Your expectations—both of yours, really—are you'll have a straightforward conversation and there's no judgment on either side.

Another thing that sounds simple but probably isn't is adjusting your own behavior. We all had that one friend in middle school who lied about everything. Heck, maybe it was you. Eventually, that person got caught in their web, and nobody wanted to talk to them. Take that lesson to heart, and stop the little white lies and all else. Be honest, and good things will come to you.

I'm not saying any of this is going to be easy for you. It's certainly been a learning experience for myself, as it has for other teammates, and we definitely make mistakes. But believe me, this is a huge step in the right direction. You just have to take the moment to accept that you will make mistakes on the path, but it'll all be good in the end.

STUFF WORTH REMEMBERING

At the end of the day, it all comes down to speaking the truth.

By being candid with our thoughts, we're also showing

our clients and fellow teammates that we are honest and not holding anything back. This creates a climate where trust is foremost, and nobody thinks that anyone else is skirting the truth just to get ahead. It solves disagreements sometimes before they even happen, and it makes sure everyone is on the same page.

Candor is critical to an organization like ours, and without it, we would not be where we are today—and it certainly would not have been nearly as much fun getting there.

Tips for Establishing Candor

1. Leadership Modeling and Training

   □ *Leading by Example*: It's imperative that senior leadership and management model candor in their interactions. When employees see their leaders practicing open and honest communication, everyone believes it is real.

   □ *Training*: Offer training sessions or workshops on the benefits and methods of candid communication. Role playing is the best training.

2. Create Safe Channels for Open Communication

   □ *No-Retaliation Policy*: Emphasize and enforce a strict no-retaliation policy for those who speak up. Employees need to know that they can be honest without fear of negative consequences.

- □ *Anonymous Feedback Mechanisms*: Establish channels, such as suggestion boxes or anonymous digital platforms, where employees can provide candid feedback without revealing their identity.

- □ *Regular Check-Ins:* Managers should have regular one-on-one check-ins with team members to discuss any concerns, feedback, or ideas. This can foster an environment where employees feel their voice is heard. We do this through our Start, Stop, Continue (SSC) meetings, but any strategy for regular check-ins will work.

3. Cultural Reinforcements

- □ *Celebrate Candor*: Recognize and reward individuals or teams that demonstrate candor, whether it's through challenging the status quo, pointing out potential issues, or sharing new ideas.

- □ *Integrate into Hiring and Onboarding:* During the hiring process, screen for individuals who value openness and direct communication. Always educate new hires on the company's value of candor, and provide them with tools and guidance on how to practice it.

CHAPTER FIVE

NO BCD

. . . .

The person who complains about the way the ball bounces is likely the one who dropped it.

–LOU HOLTZ

M any years ago, there was a wise and compassionate priest who lived in a small kingdom ruled by a proud and arrogant king. One day, as the priest was walking through the streets, he found a beggar who was complaining intensely about his circumstances.

"Nobody ever stops to help me," the beggar said. "I'm always hungry and cold. And you know what? It's not my fault. It's the rich and powerful people like the king and his courtiers who never give to folks like me."

The priest couldn't just pass by without comment, so he settled down next to the beggar with compassion in his eyes. "Sir, let me tell you a story," he said.

He began: "Once there was a king who ruled his kingdom with great power and authority. He was feared by his enemies and respected by his people, but all was not well. The king was plagued by anxiety and worries, which kept him up all night. It was a true problem, and he needed help.

"He decided to seek the advice of a wise man in his kingdom. The king asked, 'How can I be happy and content?' The wise man gave his advice: 'Go out into the city and observe the people you see, then return.'

"The king did just that. He walked through his city, watching the lives of his citizens as he passed by. There were people who were happy even though they were poor and rich people who complained constantly and were unhappy.

"When the king returned to the wise man, now rich with the knowledge of how his people actually live, he asked, 'What is the secret to happiness?' And what the wise man responded with the king took to heart.

"'It is not what you have or what you lack that determines your happiness,' the wise man said. 'It all depends on how you think about it. If you are always blaming others for your problems, you will never be happy. But if you accept what you have an make the most of it, you will find contentment and joy.'"

The beggar listened to the priest's story and, as the priest got up and walked away, considered what he said. It was true, he had been blaming others for his own problems, and this needed to change. The beggar decided to start looking for ways to improve his own circumstances, and in time, he found happiness and contentment despite his poverty.

There is nothing to gain from blaming, complaining, and defending. Only things to lose.

The Basics

Let me start off by saying that I am not the inventor of the concept of No BCD. People have discussed the dynamics of BCD—blaming, complaining, and defending—for years. (Tim Kight of Focus 3 has refined the concept to a new level, and I would encourage everyone to seek out his content.) However, its implementation at our company, and the way it's changed our dynamics, is pretty important. It's why it's an RSi core value and a key part of this book.

So here's the basics: We don't blame, we don't complain, and we don't defend.

Think about that phrase for a minute and each of the things contained inside. You probably have an inherent understanding of what each of those words means and how they apply to you and your situation. You could probably even throw out a few examples of BCD in your own life, too. But here's the thing: You may think you get it, but it's not until you've lived it that you truly understand how much of a game changer No BCD really is, particularly here at RSi.

Plain and simple: If we do these things—blame, complain, and defend—our ability to solve problems, move agendas forward, and generally get things done is exponentially hindered. Long story short, you can get stuff done (or GSD, if the "S" means something different to you) when you practice No BCD.

But, as always, this concept is best explained through a story.

The New Client

One of the big things in the business world is client attrition. For the uninitiated, the basic concept here is attrition refers to losing clients, and in our industry, that number is 30 percent. That's a pretty significant number, and what it means is companies are constantly looking to bring in new clients to fill the void left by that 30 percent—or they work harder to keep the employees they have.

Our client attrition rate is between 5 and 7 percent, which is fantastic. We've accomplished this because we have a bullheaded focus on client retention. As with investing, rule number one for growth is to not lose anything. And, when you do have the inevitable loss, it borders on heartbreaking.

For all the practical downsides of a client loss, it also presents you with a truly insidious temptation to employ BCD. And that's the scenario we were presented with when one of our core clients started looking like they were going to contribute to our attrition rate. Let's call them ABC Health System, for the sake of the story.

One of the things we did at ABC Health is something we do with all of our clients. First, we did our best to do a fantastic job of what they are asking us to do. But we also went above and beyond by spending a lot of time with their management, from all levels. We knew the chief financial officer (CFO), VP, director, and assistant director—everyone we could talk to, really—both on the administrative side and on the operation side. The idea behind this being if you lose one of those people—either their support or they literally leave the company—we have others who believe in us and our work. It's worked well for us over the years and did work well at ABC Health Until it didn't, anyway.

Then the VP over at ABC Health decided to leave. OK, no worries, no big deal. We still had connections with everyone else, so we should be fine. But then the director left, along with two of our four points of contact, both of which were pretty critical. So when the CFO decides to retire, we know we might have a problem on our hands.

Sure enough, we did. ABC Health's new CFO hired a new director, and that director had their own ideas about how they should provide these services. Through that and so many other trials and tribulations, we ended up losing ABC Health as a client, which, in this case, meant we had three months left in our contract and we were done.

This was obviously a big deal for us, so what we did around here was a postmortem. The idea was to break down what went right and wrong with the company in question, so we could learn everything we could from the process.

At that point, there was plenty of blame that could go around. And you can understand why, right? Losing that client was a big deal for the company, and when problems happen, the first thing that usually happens is people point fingers. "Well, if Susan in accounting hadn't screwed up that invoice, we would be fine right now," and so on.

But, we didn't. Instead, we weren't defensive either internally or with the client, and we didn't blame others. Instead, we collectively came together and realized we could have done better in a few areas. We then listed those out and came up with solutions for them in the future. We wanted to depart our relationship with that client with our head held high, let them know that we're proud of our work with them, and we're happy to help them transition to a new vendor. We then spent the next three months working with ABC Health like they were going to be our client for the next ten years, even though the end was in sight.

During those three months, we saw our replacements come in as new vendors. Three companies would do the job we had done before, and, true to our word, we helped ABC Health transition to these new organizations. This earned us the trust and respect of their new

VP and CFO, which made the end much more amicable. Frankly, it went as well as it could have under the circumstances.

Two years later, all four of our contacts at ABC Health had moved on to other companies for various reasons. The assistant director moved to another company and became a director; the director became a director at yet another organization; the VP became a revenue cycle VP at a larger facility; and the CFO stayed a CFO, just with a new health system.

Today, as a result of our ability not to blame, complain, or defend, three of those four members of management are now our clients. And that fourth one? He's bringing us to their new organization, too. They all want to continue doing business with RSi.

Things could have gone a lot differently. There was definitely a time in our company's history when we would blame our clients for any problems, issues, or general breakdowns that happened along the path as we were on our way out of the contract, complained internally and externally about the situation, and defended our position for one reason or another. But because we didn't blame, we didn't complain, and we didn't defend, we did the best thing to do in that scenario: our job. That made the difference between losing one client forever and turning that loss into a gain of four.

Blaming

Do you have any kids? I've got two—both boys—and over the years I've heard each of them blame the other for whatever was causing them problems at the time. And it's easy enough to see why, particularly when it's coming from a child.

Let's put this into context. Say my eldest son was walking through the house, tripped on one of his little brother's toys, and, in the process of trying to catch himself as he fell, put a hole in the drywall. He's not hurt, but he's mad. And he also knows he doesn't want to be the one to be responsible for patching that hole. He doesn't want to get in trouble, so his mind races trying to figure out whose fault it is other than his own. Wait. Didn't he trip over his little brother's toy? Well, none of this would've happened if that wasn't there; therefore, it's his little brother's fault that the wall has a hole in it. Time to tell the folks.

If you have kids, then you've heard some variation of this story more than enough times. Child A blames Child B for something because Child A not only doesn't want to get into trouble but also doesn't want to accept responsibility for their actions.

And even if you don't have kids, you probably know a person or two like this. They're usually a snake oil salesperson of some kind, promising solutions that never come, and then blame the results on you or someone else. "Well, you would've lost 10 lb. of fat if you had taken my snake oil with milk instead of water," for example.

You could even look into your own past and see examples of when you played the blame game yourself. You didn't cause that car crash; they were talking on their phone. And your adjusting of the stereo at the same time had nothing to do with it.

The blame game is universal. We've all done it, whether it's to someone else or ourselves, and we need to stop the process entirely.

Blaming other people is a toxic trait, and nobody likes to be the recipient.

To figure out how to get past this problem, you have to look at the underlying cause.

You've likely heard of impostor syndrome. If not, here's the basics. Say you get a promotion, but once you're in the role, you feel like you definitely don't belong. There's no way you should have this position; you're just a kid from Springfield or wherever. It's a level of insecurity that seems totally rational to the person experiencing it, and yet sometimes it's very much not the case.

Now what does this have to do with blaming? In this scenario, where a person is experiencing imposter syndrome, they may feel overly defensive. That causes them to deflect blame onto other people, if only as a mode of self-preservation. That can absolutely work, which encourages the imposter syndrome victim to repeat that process.

This is just one manifestation of our insecurities laid bare, and when that happens, it's easy to play the blame game. Why not point the finger at someone else? It throws the attention away from yourself, which keeps you feeling nice and cozy where you're at. Pay no attention to that man behind the curtain.

A lot of people use blame to defend themselves. Say you're in an argument with your significant other. You prepared this nice dinner, but you forgot about something in the oven and it burned. They get home late, so you pin the blame on them. "I got all frazzled when you didn't get home on time, so the food got burned." Your spouse didn't do anything wrong, while you did, so you shift the blame in their direction.

How about at work? Happens all the time, particularly with teams and team projects. Paige didn't get one thing done on time; therefore, the project isn't in. Not your fault, right? Even though you didn't do any of the required work on your end? Paige becomes the scapegoat, while you sit there looking innocent.

Another reason? Responsibility. It's hard out here sometimes to just own up to what you did, whether it's good or bad. Here's an example: Say I didn't get this book you're reading off to my editor on time, and they're mad. Totally understandable. I screwed up, so I should accept that and move forward. Not everyone does, though. It's why the "dog ate my homework" excuse was so popular when I was a kid. Telling someone else you made a mistake feels really, really bad. Why would you put yourself through that if you didn't have to? Particularly if there's someone or something you can blame it on?

And look, it sucks to say this, but it has to be said: People lie. Whatever the reason, people will just lie to get out of what they see as a bad situation. People lie, and it's not great, but sometimes that lie becomes placing blame on someone else.

Once you know why you or someone else is blaming another person or thing, then you can figure out how to solve the problem. Usually that means explaining about the root causes, like accepting responsibility. Then they have to determine what they want to do about it.

In our case, the important part is to never start blaming. It's the first part of No BCD, and one could argue the most important one. People who come into a role here learn pretty quickly that we won't play the blame game. They just have to decide whether or not they want to play the game more than they want a job.

Complaining

Now since complaining is the second part of No BCD, it would seem to imply they're two different things. It turns out, not so much.[5]

Take a moment, and think about the concept of complaining. What are you really doing? Quick example: You walk into the office, and the trash hasn't been taken out. So now you start complaining about the smell from last week's lunch that's sat in there over the weekend. Are you just complaining about the smell, or is what you're really doing blaming the person why they didn't take out the trash?

---

5   Neil Farber, "To Complain or Blame: Is That the Question?," *Psychology Today*, November 23, 2010, https://www.psychologytoday.com/us/blog/the-blame-game/201011/complain-or-blame-is-the-question.

And that's the interesting part. Many times you can't complain about something without simultaneously blaming someone else. The two things work hand in hand, and I bet you never thought of things that way before because I sure haven't.

Now this means that should you find a way to stop blaming people for other things, then the complaining should go away as well. And although that's a good way to think about it, you're not always going to be able to scratch complaining off the list entirely. Sometimes it's just bred into who you are, right?

We all know people like that. They're just negative personalities who love to moan about whatever problem is hitting them today, even if it's not important. They're pessimists, and although that's not a great way to live, it's gotten them this far, so they might as well push forward with the same behaviors.

They might have good reasons, too. A bad childhood or just general poor luck is a good enough reason for some people to feel like the world is against them. If you were to label these folks, it would be as a chronic complainer.[6] They're not focusing on the good stuff that happens to them every day and instead spend a lot of time and effort on the bad.

Then there's another type of complaining, which is kind of stealthy. It's called "venting," and I'm sure you've done that before, most likely to your significant other. "Can you believe it? Grant never took out the trash, so I came in with my office smelling like last week's salmon!" It's a pressure relief valve for people to use to just let off steam, as it were. And that's great—we all need a way to do that. But venting is really just a variation of the same old type of complaining

---

6   Robert Biswas-Diener, "The Three Types of Complaining," *Psychology Today*, June 20, 2017, https://www.psychologytoday.com/us/blog/significant-results/201706/the-three-types-complaining.

we all know and love. And if we're doing this to people who are very familiar with the situation—coworkers and the like—then what we're really doing is looking for validation. If the coworkers nod their head in agreement, then we know we're right for feeling the way we do.

Let's break down the final one though, which is called an "instrumental complaint,"[7] and it's a little bit tricky. Basically, you're complaining but still working things out to solve a problem. See, usually a complaint is just you griping about whatever happens to be wrong that day—"Old man yells at cloud," to reference *The Simpsons* and all that. But instrumental complaining starts with the problem and then rolls into how you can fix it.

You could look at an instrumental complaint as a positive thing, and you're not necessarily wrong. After all, you're working to solve a problem, and that's a good thing. But the first part, the complaining, can still have some negative side effects, and that's also something to consider. So, on the one hand, yes, you're attempting to fix something that's broken, but on the other, you're not doing it in the most constructive way.

For our purposes, pointing out a deficiency, an error, or an issue is not complaining. We want to know if we can improve. If we don't know about a concern, we can't fix it. However, we have our requirement: when you find deficiencies, issues, errors, or concerns, first, bring them to someone who can actually do something about it, and second, give them an opportunity to fix it. Repeatedly talking about the same issues without seeking a solution or talking to people who can't fix it, is, by definition, the "C" in BCD.

So what's so bad about complaining, anyway? If we're venting, we're using a complaint as a pressure relief valve. If we're doing it all

---

7   Ibid.

the time, well, maybe things are just always bad, right? Maybe these complaints are the only way anything's going to get done?

Here's the main reason why we shouldn't be complainers, regardless of the why: it's a morale killer. It, in the words of Jeff Spicoli from *Fast Times at Ridgemont High*, "harshes the good vibes." It makes others feel bad, even if they did nothing wrong. It's certainly not productive; if you think complaining is going to get your problem fixed, you're probably wrong. It's more likely that things will not go the way you planned or expected.

It's why we believe so strongly in the concept of No BCD. If we stop the complaining and focus on the good instead, good things will happen.

Defend

Let's tackle the last letter in No BCD, which is all about defending. The goal here is for you not to get defensive or to feel like you have to defend yourself. And while those two things sound like they're the same, they're not, and we need to break it down.

Let's start with being defensive with, per usual, an example. You know how sometimes you'll go for a walk and see someone with their dog? And it's a super cute animal, so you want to pet it—but the dog isn't having any of it, so they put their tail between their legs, rear back, and sit to show they definitely don't want you anywhere near their business. If you do continue, you might get bit, and you should expect that. After all, they're just being defensive.

This is one of the ways that you can also act, particularly if either the B or C part of BCD is in play. "Grant didn't take out the trash, so now my office smells like fish." Sure, but what if you're Grant? You could have a quick retort: "Well, I would've taken out the trash if you hadn't locked the door when you left early at noon." Ooh, sick burn.

In that situation David is being defensive, and really, you probably think he's right to do so. But now it's perpetuating the problem. The first person complained, which involved blaming someone else. And now Grant is defending himself, but that also flips around the attack and could even contain some blaming and complaining of its own. And the cycle could continue, with defensiveness and blaming contained therein, too. Round and round we go, right? To put this a different way, if you've got a cake made of blaming and complaining, then defending is the icing.

Let's take a moment to examine why this all happens in the first place but from a deeper level and more from a psychological perspective. We get defensive for a lot of reasons.

We get defensive to put our mistakes in the rearview mirror. We can do this by putting the onus on someone else to take the stress off our shoulders. It wasn't us who caused the problem (even if we secretly worry that it was), but it was the other person. Once that's sorted, we're not only in the clear but also coming out ahead—or at least we think we are.

Defensiveness also comes in other forms. It occurs when we look at who we are and compare ourselves to others. In this way we can warp reality to make it seem like we're better than we actually are. We can use other coping mechanisms as a form of defensiveness to keep the bad thoughts away. The problem with all of these is that it also keeps your friends, family, and coworkers at arm's length. What they're seeing is someone who doesn't know how to manage their own feelings and is always blaming things on others. It's the Chicken Little syndrome in real life. Yet the defensive person will just keep on digging no matter what and will get deeper and deeper into that hole.

There's a lot of insecurity wrapped up in defensiveness, and you need to tackle that head-on prior to anything else. A lot of times, we get defensive either because we know we did something wrong and we don't want to fess up, or because it exposes one of our insecurities. Both of those can be difficult to deal with, because really, who wants to do all that self-exploration? But if instead you start looking at yourself, examining your values, and understanding your insecurities, you won't jump to being defensive. After all, once you know who you really are, there's no reason to pin the blame on anyone or anything else. It's easier just to admit you're wrong (which also goes back to candor).

Think about phrases deep in the cultural vernacular. One we all know: "Haters gonna hate." Another one I've heard is, "If you're not getting sued, you're not doing something right," and while that is a double negative, I'm not the one who said it, so don't sue me.

The idea here is people will always criticize what you do if they're envious of what you're doing. Think about the guy who's a successful singer and how many other singers who aren't at that point in their career talk crap about what the successful one is doing. They're feeling validated in their feelings, but when you hear about them, you might start to feel poorly about yourself—and get defensive in the process.

It's easy to say, "Just don't do that," but it's really not *that* easy. You need to believe in yourself and your actions, no matter what they are. Step up, and accept responsibility for the decisions you've made. After all, if you're always in charge of what you do, there's no reason to have to defend yourself. Being ruthlessly consistent about taking personal responsibility is the anecdote to defending.

You can flip the idea of being defensive into being more successful. Say you're the head of your department at work, and you're up for yet another promotion. You don't get it, but someone beneath you does. You're hurt, but you can take it in two ways. You can blame the other person, the interviewer, your manager, whoever, and defend yourself and your actions. Or you can instead look at ways to make yourself and how you work better. Don't waste your energy doing all this defending and blaming nonsense. Instead, put it into figuring out what it'll take to get better and be a better manager—or whatever it is you do. That's taking responsibility, big time.

Admittedly, this is not going to work in every situation. After all, bad things do happen, and maybe you actually did deserve that promotion and someone else got it for nefarious reasons. Still, blaming them or the other people isn't going to change the situation. It is what it is. Focusing on making yourself better is truly the only outcome.

If you find that you're one of those people who springs into action to defend yourself, next time take a step back and sit for a spell. Give it an hour, day, week, or more to respond. Allow your body to relax and really take stock of who you are and what you're worried about. In this way you won't automatically defend yourself and instead will soothe your ego and sort out the right way to solve the problem.

Now here's the biggie, at least according to the experts. If you want to stop being defensive, use "I" statements.

Think about how you talk when you're being defensive. "You did this," or "You were the one to screw that up." But if instead you say something like, "I'm not happy with how this happened" or "I'm having a hard time coping with the situation right now because of the way I'm interpreting what you say," then you're not defending. You're now slowing down the momentum of the argument and making things run a ton smoother. Sometimes slower is better, and when it comes to being defensive, this falls into that category.

No matter which approach you take or however you handle things, the key thing to take away here is not to get defensive.

Two Trainees

Back when COVID-19 first hit, we ran into a snag. Our business could keep going remotely, but to make sure it could smoothly meant a lot of things had to go into place. One of them was training. We had to determine how to get an online-only training team up and running, and then get them to perform regularly. It was definitely going to be a challenge.

Week one rolled up, and while it's running, we figured out that we had to find some way to determine how well things were going or not. We decided to do a poll of the new trainees at the end of each week and gave them a 1–10 scale, with 10 being the best and 1 being the worst. It was a four-week course, everyone would get the same questionnaire, and the same people were polled each week.

Well, once the week was done, we sent out the questionnaire and went through the results. Almost everyone responded somewhere between a 6 and an 8, with one 10 and one 1. Great. We filed that away and moved forward.

Week two happens, and we got a lot more 8s, a few 6s, a few 10s, and one 1. Week three saw more improvement as well.

Then we came up to week four. Now we got four 10s, three 8s, and one 1. Huh. There was that 1 again. Weird.

It was time to do some analysis.

Looking at the outliers gave us the best perspective. For week one, the person who rated it a 10 loved the instructor. "It was amazing. They did such a great job! I never would have guessed it was their first time!" Super positive and upbeat, just like you'd expect.

Then there was the 1. "The trainer was completely unprofessional. I immediately regretted signing up for the organization." Wow. That's a lot to process.

Now it was the reviews for week two, and in this situation, there were some computer login issues that prevented the training class from starting on time for multiple days. An annoyance for sure. However, IT jumped into the fray immediately, but because it was a unique situation, they had to call the software vendor to figure out what they could do to resolve the issue. The trainer was transparent with the class and made sure to keep everyone informed.

Again, we had two different perspectives. From the 10: "It was amazing to see them spring into action and how committed they were to my success, even though I've only been here a week, so I rated them a 10. I was just amazed." And from the 1: "It didn't work, number one, which is not good. Number two, the IT guy couldn't fix it. Number three, they had to resort to calling the manufacturer of the software and it was crazy."

Each person had the same scenario, lived through the exact same thing, and both had completely different perspectives. Neither one of them was lying, as they both had the same set of facts in front of them. It just was how they looked at it.

The following two weeks had the same kind of results and the same kinds of answers from the 10s and the 1. Now we did this test blind, so we didn't know who was who, but the 1 wrote and complained about similar things along the way. Meaning that one of our trainees was not going to work out. They were what we call a "BCDer." They blame, complain, and defend.

Now we didn't go hunt down that person and fire them. Instead, we knew it would work itself out, and, sure enough, it did. The person who rated things a 1 consistently ended up quitting shortly thereafter as they were unsatisfied with the role. And you know what? That's totally fine. I don't want to force you to live my values any more than

I would want you to force me to live by yours. If it's not a good fit, then it's not a good fit.

But we learned something that day. We now knew that having No BCD as a value was truly valuable to the organization, and staying true to that meant we would lose some people along the way. But those who stay will just help us make the organization stronger as a whole.

Stopping the Cycle

The easiest way to stop doing these behaviors is predicated on two things: recognition and decision.

First, you have to be aware. It's pretty easy to see negative traits in other people, but it's harder to look inside and see what we're responsible for in our own lives. This takes a little bit of soul searching sometimes, plus some tough talk with yourself. Honesty can be difficult to wrangle, particularly if you're dealing with something you did that you wished you hadn't. Recognize and call yourself out when you blame, complain, defend, or generally whine about the state of things.

Once you do some self-reflection, it's now time to make some decisions. The first obvious one is to consciously stop BCDing. Don't blame, complain, or defend. Instead, take a different action that can solve the problem.

For example, let's say you and your coworker are on a project, and they completely drop the ball. It's their fault, but you're not going to BCD your way out of this problem. Instead, you could have a conversation with the coworker about the issue. Maybe they'll step up and accept responsibility. Or they could have a completely different perspective and think you're the real issue to be dealt with. A conversation could sort out the issue without any BCDing at all.

Whatever you decide to do, you need to move forward toward a resolution of some form or fashion. When you're working on the problem, you're not BCDing. You're making progress, one way or another, and nobody gets hurt.

All that said, sometimes there are problems that we're not able to solve. That's OK. In those instances, after we recognize there is no solution, we move forward and grind through the issue. Be resilient. Be tough and grind forward with all the grace and the gratitude you can muster and know that this, too, shall pass.

It's not a very sexy answer, but it's a very real one.

STUFF WORTH REMEMBERING

Blaming, complaining, and defending are like a cancer to an organization. If you have one, the others follow, and things get real messy, real quick.

Stopping the BCD cycle is critical to getting your organization, or the one you belong to, running at max efficiency. If you don't, you're going to see a lot of finger pointing and much less getting done.

Tips for Breaking the BCD Cycle

1. It Starts with ALL of US

   □ *Leading by Example:* Everyone should actively demonstrate the value by taking ownership of their mistakes, focusing on solutions rather than dwelling on problems, and refraining from defending their actions unnecessarily. This sets the tone for the rest of the organization.

   □ *Workshops:* Conduct workshops that educate employees about the negative impacts of BCD behaviors and the benefits of positive alternatives. Discuss live, real examples.

2. Accountability Mechanisms

   □ *Root Cause Analysis:* Instead of placing blame when things go wrong, implement a system where the focus is on understanding the root cause of the issue and finding solutions.

   □ *Performance Reviews:* Integrate the value of "Not Blaming, Complaining, or Defending" into performance evaluations.

3. Cultural Reinforcements and Recognitions

   □ *Storytelling:* Yes, we are going to keep using this one! Share stories of instances where employees displayed the opposite of BCD behavior, highlighting the positive outcomes that resulted. This can be done in company newsletters, team meetings, or internal communications platforms.

   □ *Small Group Activities:* Organize team-building exercises or challenges that emphasize positive collaboration and problem-solving, reinforcing the idea that teams achieve more when they work together without resorting to BCD-ing.

CHAPTER SIX

TEAM OVER INDIVIDUAL

There are no problems we cannot solve together, and very few that we can solve by ourselves.

–LYNDON B. JOHNSON

In the early 2000s, there were two men who decided to start a business together. They saw an opportunity to get into the medical equipment field, as they had a patent on a particularly unique piece of technology that would revolutionize patient care. And so, with a dream in mind, they decided to start on the road to success.

Their first hire was an engineer; naturally they needed someone to create this product, so a person who understood Computer-Aided Design (CAD) and special software called SolidWorks was important to the creation of this whole thing. Then they hired a second, and, in a fit of optimism, hired a shipping department manager to ship out the products they hadn't even created yet.

Oh, have I not talked about the owners? I probably should, because these two guys were quite interesting. The first, we'll call him Isaac, was ostentatious. He was in his mid-fifties, losing his hair, yet still somewhat fit. Every day he wore a collared shirt with the Ferrari horse on the chest, which matched the car he drove regularly to the office. His Ferrari's keys were always kept at the edge of the desk, closest to the door, where anyone who came in to speak would see immediately. He was, as my mother used to tell me, "a 'New Money' man," which meant that he had earned his money himself and not come into it through generational wealth, which meant he wanted to show it off. And that he did in spades.

The other owner, let's say his name was Ted, was quite the opposite. Ted was not New Money but instead Old Money. He was rich because his parents were rich, as were his grandparents. He was also in his mid-fifties but a bit on the heavy side with shoulder-length hair. He often wore sweaters that were just slightly worn and drove a mid-1990s Land Rover every day. He also owned a Ferrari, but his was a classic—a Testarossa—that he only drove on special occasions. He was a connoisseur, you see, and he didn't feel the need to show off his wealth. Instead, he was content to be the primary money man in this whole operation.

As the engineers worked on this medical marvel, they did what engineers did and made things difficult. The specs for the machine required very precise measurements—within 0.001 of an inch—which meant all of the parts would have to be manufactured somewhere with those capabilities and not in-house. This would normally not be a problem, but Isaac and Ted wanted to get a prototype out into the world to pitch to investors and hospitals. Precise was good, but good was also good enough.

Eventually, parts came in, and now the shipping manager was assigned with putting the thing together. He tried, but with just hand tools and a drill, it was impossible to reach the perfecting standards of the engineers. In fact, it became so much of a problem that the shipping manager quit in frustration, leaving the group without someone to assemble their lone product, and a pair of smug engineers who thought they had all the solutions in the world.

Isaac and Ted realized that the problem here was the team. Each person thought they were working in a vacuum—even the two engineers—and wanted to see their own success over the others in the group. This wasn't a functioning group, and the owners needed to make a change.

The pair decided it was time to scrap the whole team and start over. But this time, instead of getting the people they needed, they decided to start with their values. Isaac and Ted wanted to establish what the actual goals of the company were and then hire accordingly. The people they would bring in would know from the jump what the company believed in, how they wanted to operate, and what their mission was.

Oh, and their most important value? "The whole is greater than the one." Or, to put it another way, Team over Individual.

One or All?

One of the things we talk about a lot here at RSi is the concept of Team over Individual (often shorthanded as a math equation, Team>Individual). Anyone that's ever played a sport understands this idea, and even if you've never changed in a locker room, you probably know the fundamentals. Basically, no one person is better than anyone else when it comes to the team as a whole, and our success is only what we can accomplish together.

The concept highlights the importance of cooperating as a team to accomplish shared goals and objectives. I'll talk more about those goals in a minute, but expanding things out further, individual accomplishments pale in comparison to the performance of the team as a whole. And furthermore, the collaborative efforts and contributions of *all* team members are crucial to the organization's success.

I'm going to put this into a sports context, because that's really the best way to go. Let's talk about Michael Jordan again. One of the best basketball players of all time, arguably to this day. It was obvious that at any point he could take over a game and win it for the group. But it's also debatable whether or not he could win a game or a championship without that surrounding team. A good example of this is when he played for the Washington Wizards. You could argue that he was no longer in his prime, sure. But either way, all of his championship rings come from the Bulls, not the Wizards—because he didn't have that team to back him up.

The same rules apply to one of today's biggest stars, LeBron James. He couldn't carry the Lakers on his shoulders in the 2021–2022 season, and they flopped hard. No matter how well he played, if he didn't have the support of his team, he failed.

Let's put that into our framework then. At RSi, we cluster people into teams, and each team has a goal. For example, say we've got five people on a team, and their goal is to generate $5 million in revenue for this particular client. One person could be the rockstar of the group and produce $4 million, while two collect $500k each, and the last two get nothing. In that scenario, the entire team still earns a bonus because they met their goals.

Now that seems weird on the surface, right? But here's the thing: Some people shoot the shots, while others make the assists. As long as they're all performing well, you've got a good team on your hands.

But why? Well, that's because of one of the other components baked into our Team over Individual concept: motivation.

Motivation

Let's take a moment to face facts. RSi is a BPO with a large call center component, and about a third of our operation is focused on collecting money from people or companies who owe it to our healthcare provider clients. When one of our teammates puts on their headset every day, they know whoever they call doesn't want to talk to them. And, chances are, they're going to be unpleasant to deal with. As for the remaining two-thirds, they too have to deal with people who aren't necessarily excited to hear from us like insurance companies or attorneys.

As a result, turnover in this industry is high, and we understand why. Calling people who aren't the most excited to hear from you is not the ideal job for everyone. But for those who do stay, we don't want them to burn out. Nobody wants to come in every day knowing they'll deal with horrible things. Motivation, therefore, is key.

This motivation comes in a lot of forms. Obviously, compensation plays a huge role in keeping people focused and energized. While we like to think everyone is enjoying the job, if we weren't paying well, it's likely we'd have far fewer people showing up at the office every Monday morning. While every team and department are somewhat different, we always tie the performance success of the group to the financial success of the individual. This means when the clients win (by us achieving *their* goals), RSi wins, the team wins, and all the contributing team members are rewarded. In addition, individuals have the opportunity to earn bonuses or commissions outside of the team structure, but these are typically one half of the team bonus. This is absolutely by design. We want to make 100 percent sure our reward system matches our values and the behavior we are encouraging.

Compensation, though, isn't enough. Our employees need other forms of motivation, and that's where the team comes in.

Walk into one of our on-site call centers, and you're going to see a hub of activity. People standing up at their desks, maybe pacing while on a call, or just stretching their legs. Our remote teams are hyping up members of the group with their strong emoji game on chat or by giving them virtual pats on the back. There's a lot of camaraderie in our operations centers, and that's because of teamwork. The idea of "being in this together" can be felt on a team even if we aren't in the same room.

Within our operation, each person is a part of a small team of ten to twelve people. And just like many other organizations, that team is a part of a larger team as well, and up the chain it goes. They've got lots of people there for support, whether it's a buddy to bend an ear to at lunch or a manager to help with problems on a call. And like any work scenario, you're going to make some friends on the job, too.

By focusing on the team and the importance of that structure, we're building them a little work family. Those family members help motivate the team and keep it cohesive. It's critical in demonstrating how we prioritize the Team.

The support system that's built up between team members creates a sense of community. It's hard to understate how important that is, particularly in our industry and in this current environment. Team over Individual sets the tone for our actions, our words, and our attitudes. New associates see this and fall in quickly, knowing they'll soon be giving the reinforcement others are receiving now.

Now when I say that, I don't mean that we're propping people up one way or another. Instead, it's about team members supporting one another both emotionally and otherwise. Say you get off a tough call and you're debating whether or not you could see yourself doing this job anymore. Then your buddy pops online and gives you that pick-me-up that you needed. Or you chat with the rest of your team and find out they're all having rough days, too. So you commiserate together and eventually do a happy hour (virtual happy hour and morning coffee sessions have become incredibly popular) to lift everyone's spirits. By the end of the day, you're revitalized and ready to hit it again in the morning.

Engagement

Now from a leadership angle, this has another advantage. Keeping your employees engaged can be tough. You want them to be motivated to do things, sure. But you also want them to actively care about what they do and their end result. Look, we're not necessarily concerned with how we get to the finish line, but we obviously want productive people.

When individuals prioritize the team's well-being above their own, it demonstrates a deep commitment and sense of responsibility. By having skin in the game, they show a personal investment in the team's success and a willingness to take ownership of their actions and decisions. Putting your team's interests first creates an environment of collaboration and support. Individuals recognize that achieving success relies on collective (pun absolutely intended) effort and are willing to go the extra mile to contribute effectively.

This same engagement also turns into efficiency. Think about a world where we could take a few people, smush their combined knowledge into one place, and then ask questions to that super brain of theirs. This is effectively what happens with a great team. The entire group can work as one, using all of their experiences to come up with solutions to problems. You get better problem-solving, decision-making, and innovation. And, as a bonus, you also gain new procedures and ways of doing things, all created by the efficiency built into this new team structure.

This kind of scenario is another really cool one when you bring on a new employee. They can sit with (virtually or otherwise) the combined knowledge of the group and not only feel like they're a part of the team but also know they're in good hands. The elder teammates of the group can guide the new person along the path, and it reduces anxiety on all parts. The team functions as a group.

Collaboration

This approach has a ton of advantages, particularly when you're working with a team like ours. One of the big ones? A sense of collaboration.

Maybe you've worked in a call center–type environment before, or maybe you haven't. Let me just take a moment to paint the picture for you. There's a big room, and there are tons of cubicles, each one with a workstation, phone, headset, and a comfy chair. In those seats are employees, and they're working with customers one way or another. Sometimes it's a customer service thing, sometimes it's scheduling or insurance claims follow-up, and other times it's collections. No matter which one it is, they're on the phone for large chunks of the day.

Now our goal is to cultivate an environment where our teammates can have fun and actually enjoy their work. Nobody should have to drag themselves to work each day. They should look forward to their tasks and understand their contribution. Even better, if they have friends on their team and they know the energy of the work is going to be infectious, well they're all in. They want to do their best job so that everyone on their team will do their best, too.

This concept is particularly critical with remote workers. These are the team members who may have never seen the inside of our facility, nor will they ever. To bring them into the mix, we use collaboration as a tool. Those shared goals and objectives take someone who's working remotely and help them feel like they're in the room with everyone else. Sure, there are no high fives when the goals are hit, but there are plenty of both planned and spontaneous celebrations.

Collaboration also brings with it a certain amount of energy. I've found, in my professional life, that nearly all good things I've done came when I was working with someone else. I may act like a toddler on a sugar bender at times, but I can't do everything by myself. Neither can anyone, which is why working with other people helps us all get things done. It's the same way for our team, no matter where they're working.

Mutual Respect

Between all of the other team-related things I've talked about so far, one of the big parts that not only encourages the others but also keeps people wanting to work here is the idea of mutual respect.

There is no one person on a team that's better than the others. Because they can all combine into this giant robot that's bigger than it's individual parts, they know that together they can do amazing things. But it also means they all can respect one another equally. There's no infighting because of jealousy or anything along those lines, because they're all on the same team, and they are pulling for one another. We win together!

It's absolutely not easy, but think about all of the problems that solve for both bosses and employees. There's far less stress coming into the office because of performance issues or whatever, because the group works together as a unit. If someone falls down, the team picks them back up together. It's pretty great stuff when practiced consistently.

That's not all. Employees are more likely to feel appreciated and supported when their efforts are respected and acknowledged. And that tracks, right? Because I'm sure that you have been in situations where you don't feel like you've been appreciated. Or that you're not respected within the company, and I hear you. I've been there myself, and it's not a comfortable situation to find yourself in.

All of this is a huge contributor to the development of a positive and inclusive work environment. That's all we want as employees, employers, and clients. I'm betting it's one of your goals as well.

Customer Satisfaction

At the end of the day, as important as our employees are to us, there is another component here, which is our clients. Without them we'd all be out of jobs, and nobody wants that for sure. But as much as you wouldn't think it would be the case, Team over Individual also has a pretty substantial effect on customer happiness and service.

You've probably called a support line before for your computer, or maybe it was just to get your cable bill paid on time. Whatever the situation, if you got someone grumpy on the other end of that phone line, you felt it, and our customers do, too. Think about it: You make a phone call to see if you can shave ten dollars off your monthly bill for your cell phone, and when the customer service agent on the other line picks up the phone, and there's an audible sigh at the other end, you know *right* away that nobody there wants to help you. They've got something going on that's messing up their attitude, and it's going to affect how they do their job with you.

It also means that the group brain I was talking about earlier is in full effect. When a customer has a concern, if the team member who takes the call doesn't have an answer, they can go to the team for help. It's a great way to get those issues resolved quickly and effectively. And what does that do? It develops enduring connections with our clients and goes a long way toward making them part of the team.

STUFF WORTH REMEMBERING

I could tell you a million sports analogies, but at the end of the day, it comes down to this: No one person can lift up a team so much they can win it all. Forget Jordan or James in basketball or Brady with the NFL. If you have a team activity, then the team needs to work together; otherwise they will fail.

Success comes in a lot of forms, but for us, it's all about the group effort. It creates mutual respect among team members. You get higher engagement and deeper collaboration. And it's a motivator, too. Teams that do well get better bonuses and so on. Plus, at the end of the day, our clients benefit from the great results.

We love our stars, but by building an organization around teams and not individuals, you can see some pretty big strides forward. Yes, as hokey as it sounds (and it is really, really hokey), everyone achieves more when they work together as a team.

Tips for Fostering a Team over Individual Culture

1. Set Clear Team Goals

   ▫ *Shared Objectives:* Establish specific, measurable goals for each team tied to the organization's objectives. Ensure they are understood by all.

   ▫ *Team Accountability:* Hold teams collectively accountable for results rather than individuals. Success depends on collaboration.

2. Encourage Teamwork

   ▫ *Model Collaboration:* Leaders should demonstrate and praise cross-team collaboration, cooperation, and support.

   ▫ *No Silos:* Break down silos between teams, departments, and locations. Facilitate sharing of ideas and best practices.

3. Recognition and Rewards

   ▫ *Team Awards:* Offer incentives and recognition for achievement of team goals over individual accomplishments.

▫ *Peer Appreciation:* Provide opportunities for team members to recognize one another's contributions and support.

4. Hire for Team Players

▫ *Assess Collaboration Skills:* When hiring, evaluate candidates' ability to work in a team over individual skill proficiency.

▫ *Diversity of Strengths:* Build teams with complementary skills and strengths. Different perspectives drive innovation.

5. Team-Building Activities

▫ *Bonding Opportunities:* Facilitate activities, events, and initiatives that bring team members together to build relationships.

▫ *Personal Connections:* Take interest in team members' lives and what motivates them outside of work.

CHAPTER SEVEN

NO ROI, NO SPEND

Making money is easy. It is. The difficult thing in life is not making it, it's keeping it.

−JOHN MCAFEE

A few miles off I-10, right near the swamps of Louisiana and in between Baton Rouge and New Orleans, sat a depot packed with vehicles. They were a vehicle maintenance facility—part of a larger oil operation we'll call Oil Co. (short for Oil Company; I'm creative)— and they handled all of the trucks, cars, big rigs, and everything else that's operated by the company. There were hundreds of these things, and they all required standard maintenance like oil changes and tires, but sometimes there were emergency calls for flats or blown motors out in the field as well.

Running a vehicle maintenance facility can be a pretty taxing work. Think of it like running a Jiffy Lube for five hundred vehicles, and you see the same five hundred throughout the year. It also means that things can get behind and, eventually, just not function. When that happens, you have a solution, and it's a fleet management company.

In this scenario, when Oil Co. called the fleet management company—we'll call them FRS for Fleets R' Us, for now—they worked out a deal. Usually these types of things flow as follows. FRS gets paid a standard fee every month, called their Contracted Rate. This included all standard maintenance on the vehicles, like oil changes, miscellaneous repairs, and the like. It also included the payroll for everyone on staff, including the predetermined number of mechanics, an office manager, a facility manager, and anyone else deemed necessary. Then there were Off-Contract Services. Tires were usually in this category, as they can pop or go bad randomly or because of repeated abuse. Every scenario is different, so every "ticket" provided to the team is determined to be Contract or Off-Contract before they're started. If they're Off-Contract, they needed prior approval from Oil Co. to get started.

But before all of that work began, FRS had to come into the facility and clean it up. And boy oh boy, did they have a lot to deal with at Oil Co.

See, the previous manager wasn't very neat, and so there were all sorts of spills and dried spots that just didn't look very good. There was a cabinet full of sorted nuts and bolts that fell over, and nobody bothered to clean it up, so that was a mess. Then there was the oil change pit, which had at least an inch of sludge at the base and was clearly never cleaned up. Never mind the painted floor of the facility, which was chipping and torn.

Before any work could be done on any vehicle, FRS had to fix it all. Thousands were going to be dumped into this facility by FRS, and they didn't even own the place. How and why would they do that?

Let's tackle the "how" first. Since FRS did this regularly, they had a process in place that made things easier for all involved. They put together a team of people tailor-made to fix everything in the facility. There were regular maintenance folks who fixed everything that was broken. There was an office manager type who cleaned up the paperwork and made sure everything was ready for their replacement. Someone from corporate also came into place to oversee the whole thing, and there was even a mechanic to assess all the vehicles and at what point in the maintenance program they need to be.

They did all of this work within a week. It was tough, and there were long hours to be sure. But by the end of those seven days, the entire team was on a plane and heading back home. The facility was ready for the new team to come in—run by FRS, of course—with freshly painted floors, scrubbed and cleaned surfaces, and a stock room packed with supplies.

At this point, you might be asking the "why" question. Why would FRS dump this much time and effort into a facility that they didn't own?

As it turns out, when your facility is messy, it's harder to find things. The longer it takes for you to find a part or a tool, the more time it takes for the job to be done. That much should be fairly obvious. But what FRS wanted to do was treat the facility as if it was its own. Cleaner shops are more efficient shops, and organized offices can track what the shop does. By keeping things clean and maintaining both the vehicles and the shop, they proved to Oil Co. that they should stick around, even when their contract was up.

Basically, FRS needed to spend a lot of money up front, but their ROI was keeping the customer happy, which would, in the long term, keep FRS working on-site.

In other words, No ROI, No Spend.

Defining No ROI, No Spend

At this point in the book, you're probably thinking that a lot of these chapters seem kind of fluffy or light. They're also pretty straightforward concepts that you can get your head around pretty easily. Once you start thinking about it, candor is a pretty obvious concept, right? But No ROI, No Spend? It's not as sexy as the rest of them. Frankly, some members of management call it "our boring value," and they're not wrong. But they're also not 100 percent right, either.

No ROI, No Spend is RSi's core financial value. It basically means that we're committed to getting the best ROI possible in everything that we do, and we will always spend the money *if* there is appropriate ROI.

For clarity, let's break down the concept of ROI first, because although you might have heard of it before, it bears repeating. Say you've got a lemonade stand. You spend $2.50 on lemons and sugar, and you borrow a container to put the juice into. You have *invested* $2.50 into your business.

Now let's say you're selling the lemonade. You want $1 a cup, and you can get ten cups out of your container. All in all you'll make $10 if you sell the whole batch, which, after you subtract your investment of $2.50, leaves you with $7.50 in profit. In the most basic form, that's the return from your investment.

Thing is, we don't sell lemonade. Sometimes it's funding for a special project for a new client that we want to take on here at the office. Other times it's an initiative that's company wide and needs to go out soon. Or it could just be a financial investment in property or something similar. Whatever it is, we want to make sure we maximize our ROI on every project. Every time we consider an investment, project, initiative, or anything that will cost the company money, we put it through the No ROI, No Spend filter.

Now why is that important? Let me explain with a little bit of backstory.

I was originally the president of the company, and prior to 2019, we didn't have any outside investors. The original founders were still very active in the business and extremely active in the financial decision-making. Companies in those scenarios can operate a little bit differently. When outside investors are present, there are decision-making protocols and lots of input from multiple sources. There are many different levels of stakeholders and as many opinions available as you are willing to listen to.

Pre-2019, we were a founder-owned organization, which meant that the founder ultimately made the calls. We had to literally get approval for every expense, and there were very little rules or guiding principles other than "If it costs money, we don't need it." Now, our founders are awesome guys and were well within their rights to demand financial discipline, but that's not how RSi operates today.

In October 2019, WestView Capital Partners invested in RSi, and it really re-energized the organization. While the original owners are now investors and board members, they are no longer active in the day-to-day operations, and our financial decision-making process has changed dramatically. Our leadership team from WestView strongly believed in applying whatever resources were necessary for RSi to compete at the highest level. Now, there are plenty of places to spend money in our business. Some make sense, while others don't. It can be hit or miss. Too many misses, and we're not only not writing books, but we're not in business at all. To figure out how to generate more financial hits than misses, we needed something that defined how we want to use our funds. A guidepost, as it were, to show how we would deploy our resources. This is where No ROI, No Spend was born. Without this discipline, the other values might not even be possible. You can't have growth in your business if you don't have a business, right?

Taking ROI Further

Now you know what ROI is, and you're probably thinking that means everything is purely about the numbers. Not so, reader. In fact, the "R" in ROI can have a pretty broad scope.

Take COVID-19, for example. I've already talked about the logistics of that whole scenario and what we needed to do to get the job done. But when we had those first few discussions, the initial concern was cost. It was going to take about a half-million dollars to get people out the door. That's not a small amount of scratch to spend on a whim, but we definitely wanted to keep everybody healthy and employed. We also needed to continue operations as close to capacity as possible.

From a pure dollar perspective, moving our team from an in-house model to full or partially remote may not have made a lot of sense in the moment. Spending $500k on that transition was going to hit us hard right in the center of the wallet. And remember, back in March 2020, we as a nation thought this thing was going to breeze over in two weeks. Why spend that much money on something that could be temporary? Where was the ROI in that?

Well, you already know from previous chapters, right? By going first to remote to now a hybrid setup, we have employees who work all over the country. This gives us better coverage in different time zones and the ability to grow (see chapter 1) without needing to get bigger parking lots.

All of this adds up, and there is a financial cost involved. A spend, if you will. So how can we show that our spend does have ROI? How do we square that circle? By changing our lens just a little bit.

ROI Is More Than Financial

ROI stands for "Return on Investment," but that "R" can mean a lot of different things. To a lot of companies, it's a pure numbers game. They see something to spend on and automatically want that financial payback at the end.

Say you were a bakery, and you needed to buy an additional high capacity oven for the kitchen that will set you back around $4,000. That's a lot of money when margins are tight, but you have a few choices. If you don't get a new oven, you don't get the extra income generated from it. That means losing out on all that growth. And will you make up the money eventually? Absolutely. So it may hurt at first, but eventually it will pay for itself.

This COVID-19 remote transition didn't have an obvious financial benefit other than keeping our people working when most others weren't. But in this case, the answer was simple: Sometimes the return may not necessarily be money. It may not make a good financial case, but you know what? There's plenty of return in the goodwill that we're generating. The loyalty that we will engender among our employees. The pride in being able to make that decision for the leadership team.

The day we made the switch, we stopped all three hundred of our employees from worrying about whether or not they would have a job the next day and whether they would get sick from a virus nobody knew much about. The next day they could work in their bedrooms, DoorDash some food, and be safe.

In other words, the return was huge—it just didn't directly involve dollar signs.

Another example of this comes with what equipment we supply to our employees. Now I don't know what kind of work you do, but in my case, I carry a laptop everywhere I go. No matter where work takes me, if I have that nearby, I'm set. But our call center employees mostly sit at a desk. They need a phone, a comfortable headset, and a computer. But what about those peripherals?

The straightforward answer here is to give each person the necessary equipment to move forward. This includes the previously mentioned telephone, headset, computer, and one monitor. Emphasis on one *monitor*. This would all work great, but our folks really like having at least two monitors and, in some cases, three. It gives them one area to place their messaging app to talk to other people on their team, info on the customer on another, and so on. Basically, having that extra real estate works to their advantage.

Now, when we remotely deployed, we could have certainly gone the route of providing only the minimum amount necessary. After all, we were spending a ton already, and the teammates should be happy enough with keeping their position through an uncertain time, right? That's exactly what other companies in that scenario did, and they did it for a number of reasons. For example, we have a vendor who is one of those big tech companies. When they deployed remotely, each of their employees received the bare minimum in equipment. In fact, they were asked to provide some of their own hardware in many cases. This same company also imposed temporary pay decreases of 15 percent from the top down, all the way to the very front of the front lines.

For us, we saw a return in the midst. If our employees are happier with two or three monitors, we want to promote that. If they're more productive, there's an obvious benefit there, too. And if it saves them frustration, well look, there can be a lot of turnover in those roles because of the amount of stress they can endure. So why not get them an extra monitor? It's not *that* much money, and if it keeps someone in their role longer or makes them more efficient, that's a win for us.

The return on that is a happier teammate. One that feels like they've been invested in and have been given the tools to succeed.

ROI, therefore, can mean a lot of different things. Here at RSi, we base it on financials, sure. Our CFO would stop reading at this point if we didn't document this fact here. But sometimes ROI may be more qualitative, such as the expected effect on employee engagement, customer satisfaction, or just our reputation as a whole. All of those things have value, and while there may not be a monetary amount placed on it right at the moment, the long-term effects will pay out.

The Myth of the Equation

Ultimately, there isn't an equation for ROI for the way we do it here. However, the math behind things requires us to make decisions in a disciplined and strategic way. Let me dive into that further.

We want every decision that we make to be the right one, sure. But to do that, the discipline has to be there. It has to be. To keep it in place and in check, we do a lot of research and analysis, particularly with our bigger spends.

That's where every check ultimately starts. Before we pull the trigger on spending some cash, we want to do our due diligence. Once the decision has been made, we next go about setting clear performance goals. We set up metrics to show exactly where we expect to be and what numbers we need to hit. That part is critical.

Let's put this another way. Say your goal was to collect every G.I. Joe: A Real American Hero toy made in the 1980s and early 1990s. After a quick dive down the Wikipedia rabbit hole, you discover there were several hundred of those heroic guys, and you want one of each. So you count them up, and whatever number you come up with is the number you need to get. And obviously, you don't have to go with G.I. Joes; this could be baseball cards, generations of coins, or even stamps. The point being is there is a set number in front of you, and that's the number you have to hit for the set to be complete.

Those are metrics. And we use that same concept to determine whether or not a project or a purchase is going to be successful. Spoilers for the conclusion of this book, but when we acquired a company in January 2023, we put together a list of metrics to determine whether it was a good purchase and set out another batch of metrics to determine what success looked like. And I'll tell you what, those things are critical.

Without numbers, you have no *truly* objective measure of success. Now hear me out, because that's pretty hardcore talk for sure. But numbers show you the truth. And if you have a standard—a metric—that you're working toward or against, then you know when you've succeeded—or when you didn't.

This is key to any goal you set, whether it's personal or professional. You need some kind of way to show that you have accomplished your mission and gotten the desired outcome. Otherwise, the goal can meander on forward, never being sure if you've been successful or not. Subjectivity is not our friend in goal setting.

Now, for us at RSi, setting our targets is very much a group effort. Any project that we do takes in as many team members as is necessary and reasonable. We gather everyone together and do a research and strategy session, with the end result being determining those metrics for success as well as our various other performance goals. We come up with this data before we start executing, which means we go into the project knowing where we stand.

Prioritization

As good as our team is and no matter how well we perform, sometimes things are out of our control. The economy is a big one of those, and if things are uncertain or we just don't have enough resources, No ROI, No Spend comes in real handy. With the data in front of us and the goals ready to go, we can prioritize what's important and what isn't.

Sometimes the goals we have in mind are pretty concrete. We know how things will go moving forward, so we don't have to do too much guessing. But other times, the end result may be hazy at best. We still have goals and metrics, but we're not exactly sure whether things are going to net out in a good way.

How we act depends on all sorts of factors. If the economy is going south, we probably won't do the more risky option and stick instead with the sure thing. When times are better, we'll throw uncertain options into the evaluation mix as well.

Flexibility

Let's say that nebulous project from the last section doesn't have the best ROI. It's positive, but maybe not by much, subjectively speaking. Should we take the risk?

Well, this is where No ROI, No Spend gets really useful as a core value and a tool to manage behavior.

Once we've gone through all of the heavy lifting, made a bunch of charts, and determined what the goals could be of the project, sometimes it just doesn't work out. And in those cases, if we determine there is no or little ROI on the project, then we don't spend.

Now it's important to remember that it's not always easy to predict or measure the ROI of a project or initiative. We're not psychics over here, and sometimes things will change that are completely out of our control. Sometimes it may be necessary to take a few calculated risks to achieve long-term success—and that's OK, as long as we know that going into things. However, what we don't want to do is dive in headfirst without a plan. Risks are OK, but not unless we know what we're doing.

The Company President and ROI

Mrs. Sanders was a company president who was passionate about her business and her employees. She worked very hard to ensure that her company had a positive culture, and produced excellent results for their customers. Things were nearly always good at her company.

But one day, she hit a snag. While business had grown quickly, she now had to invest in new infrastructure to support said growth. There were a bunch of different options in front of her, making it a difficult call to choose which one would be the best place to put her company's capital.

Eventually, Mrs. Sanders whittled it down to two options:

1. Invest in a flashy new office building in a trendy part of town. This was an amazing place with all of the latest amenities. People would flock to visit, and all of the employees would love coming into the office. That, and it would make a heck of a statement for the company, and that's not a bad thing, either.

2. Upgrade the company's technology to streamline its processes and increase efficiency. This wouldn't be flashy or get a lot of media attention, but it would help the company to scale quickly and efficiently.

It was a tough call. While the building would be expensive, it would be a visible symbol of the company's success. On the other hand, upgrading their tech would help their employees work smarter, not harder, which would give them better results in the long term. And really, the more she thought about it, the more she realized that team members would be happier for longer with the new technology.

It was time to do some analysis—the best way for Mrs. Sanders to make a decision. She spent her days focusing on which option would give her the best ROI by looking at the cost of each investment while weighing it against the potential benefits to the company.

In the end, Mrs. Sanders realized that while the office building would be all kinds of awesome, the investment in new technology would have a much higher ROI in the long term. As a result, the company could scale more efficiently, reduce its costs, and provide a better experience for its customers. Plus, having that technology on hand would help the business attract top talent while still keeping current employees happy by giving them the tools they needed to do their jobs more effectively.

With the decision made, Mrs. Sanders invested in the new technology—and it paid off. The company began to grow at an even more impressive pace than before thanks to her focus on ROI relative to her goals and the commitment to her employees.

Persistent Values

This entire book is about company values. Without these six bits, RSi would not be the company it is today. As such, whenever we approach a No ROI, No Spend situation, we also have to consider another thing: Does this fit in with our core values?

Let's step back a minute and address the big picture, as we have multiple times throughout this book, with a "why" question. Why should a company have values, anyway? Is it important? It sure is. The bigger the company gets, the more voices involved with every decision. Sometimes it gets so big everything gets drowned out. One of the louder voices in the room says something should get done, so it gets done, and it may not lead us and the organization in the direction we all want to go.

Values help you sort through that noise. If someone wants to take on a project or do an initiative that doesn't fit with the company values, if it doesn't fit within the guideposts, then the project or initiative doesn't happen.

Now combine that concept with No ROI, No Spend, and you've got an advanced version of the equation going. Say you want to buy one person a celebratory gift card for accomplishing something positive. The ROI is pretty good because the person will feel better about management and so on. But what about the Team over Individual value? If the individual is not as important as the team, then we should get *everyone* on the team gift cards, because, again, the individual is not as important.

We do these kinds of value comparisons all the time. It helps us make decisions and narrow down our choices so that we're not running in circles. You have to keep persistent with your values, and that's something we adhere to very strictly.

Making an Impact

Any time you spend money on a teammate, a stakeholder, a project, a tool, or anything related to the business, you want to see a positive outcome. That is kind of a more liberal version of ROI that we adhere to, as it's not just about the money. But sometimes the impact we see isn't as narrow as you would think.

Let's start inside and work our way out. Beginning with our associates, we can see that sometimes when we spend money, we can make a positive impact with them. How about stakeholders? In some cases, that's a client, and at other times, it's other teammates. Again, making a mark sometimes requires spending some money. If we're looking at big picture stuff, we have to consider what's best for shareholders in the company. Is this going to give them confidence in our decisions and the course we are charting?

Then there's the community at large. Not a lot of companies think about ROI in those terms, but we certainly do. We could do a town event to show the people in our city that we really do care. Sometimes the policies we make affect other people, and those include members of our local area whether it's through job fairs, the location of our offices, or financial decisions.

All *Tolled*

We have to take all of these things into consideration when making a No ROI, No Spend decision. Now to some, that could be paralyzing. It could generate your fight-or-flight response for sure. But for our team, it's beneficial. We have a series of guide rails that help shape how we make our decisions. It makes it easier for us, not harder, which is part of why we push so hard to keep these values in place.

Put simply, this has guided us in many ways and helped us to make better decisions. Because we now carefully weigh the potential benefits and costs of different paths, and then make our decisions based on our expected ROI, we can maximize returns. This lets us use our resources in the most effective and meaningful way possible, both on a human level and for the business as a whole.

Sounds like exciting stuff, right? Maybe No ROI, No Spend isn't such a boring value after all.

STUFF WORTH REMEMBERING

If you're going to spend money, you should have a pretty good reason. This is a fairly universal truth, so it makes fair sense to run your business that way. But from a broader perspective, we're talking about ROI. If you want that return on investment, then you should ensure that you're spending your money in a way that supports your goals and not frivolously.

This is, of course, easier said than done. ROI is a fluid concept and does not necessarily mean financial gain. Some things you have to spend money on, like it or not. But the balance here is in those details. Pick your battles, and always determine what the ROI is and how it's measured before you spend your funds.

Tips for No ROI, No Spend

1. ROI Training and Tools

   □ *Training Programs:* Conduct regular training sessions for all relevant employees, especially decision-makers, on how to calculate and interpret ROI.

   □ *ROI Calculation Tools:* Develop simple ROI calculation tools or software that can be used across departments. Keeping it simple is the key.

2. ROI Analysis Should Be Included in Every Decision-Making Process

   □ *Determine Which Expenses Require Mandatory ROI Review:* Require that any significant spending proposal or project plan includes a comprehensive ROI analysis. This ensures that decisions aren't made purely on intuition or assumptions.

   □ *RIO Look Back:* After a project's completion or a certain period post-expenditure, conduct reviews to compare the projected ROI with the actual outcome. This will inform future actions and validate assumptions.

3. Promote Financial Accountability and Transparency

   □ *Open the Books:* Consider adopting an "open-book management" style, where employees have access to financial information. This transparency can make them more aware of the financial implications of their decisions. In many cases, this creates quick buy-in.

   □ *Reward Savers:* Create reward systems or incentives for teams or individuals who consistently demonstrate wise spending habits with strong ROI outcomes.

CHAPTER EIGHT

THE CULTURE OF A WINNING TEAM

Culture trumps everything. It trumps biology; it trumps personality; it trumps our previous education and training. Culture trumps everything because it drives our behavior. It is unspoken, automatic and almost invisible. Culture helps determine what we should or should not do in a given situation. This is what makes Culture crucial to business: the CEO cannot be physically available to influence each choice an employee must make each day. But Culture can.

—TREY TAYLOR, *A CEO ONLY DOES THREE THINGS*

A few years back, a friend of mine was on this adult basketball league in a nearby state. He was pretty good, but more of a Scottie Pippen than our friend Michael Jordan, you know? He was the guy who always helped out the other, more important guy. Problem was, that other, more important guy? He was all ego.

In fact, a lot of the team seemed to be made up of people who just wanted to relive their high school glory days. There were even some ex-NCAA players in there who washed out before they ever hit the big time. Everybody just wanted the ball to score and get attention for themselves, not the team. As a result, they never really did that well, even though many of the players were quite good.

There needed to be a change, and one year at the beginning of the season, there was. A new coach came in. He was a tall fellow, maybe six-seven or six-eight, and he used to coach at a local community college. He had a different way of looking at things with this team, and so he decided to implement his system.

First, he stated their new vision: "Win. Together." It seemed simple, but it was that second word that made the ball hogs cringe a little bit in their seats. Coach was going to drill this into them hard: They were better together, not apart. Egos were not going to fly, and they needed to be selfless with their play style.

To back this up, Coach provided a new carrot instead of a stick. Players who contributed to the team's success would get saved from running wind sprints and laps at the end of practice. They did trust exercises so that they could all learn from one another and played silly games revolving around communication so they learned to actually listen to one another.

Now while this was a fun league, a lot of the guys were super competitive and didn't appreciate getting the stick end of the bargain. But they figured they'd give it a shot. And, as the season progressed, they started to see the benefits of Coach's methods.

It turns out that you can accomplish more when you're playing as a team and not just for yourself. That guy who loved to drive the lane and try to dunk hard on every play? Seemed like if he passed it off regularly, the team would score more threes. And the guy who warmed the bench? Yeah, he was pretty good at defense, but nobody had given him a chance before. Now he was grabbing rebounds like crazy to everyone's delight.

They started getting more Ws than Ls, and soon the team saw the benefits of the system in action. Players were trusting one another more. Communication was on point (see what I did there), and everyone was touching the ball. Ultimately, it was more fun for everyone, and even when they had a loss, they took it in stride. No biggie, there was always next week.

Eventually, the team made it to the playoffs. And while they didn't win the first year, nobody felt bad about it. Instead they continued to play together for another five years, ultimately winning a championship in that last season.

Here's the thing: That same group could have won a championship much earlier had they not been focused on themselves as individuals. But because Coach came in and made it about culture and not individuals, the team as a whole succeeded.

If you practice teamwork, selflessness, and a shared commitment to success, you're more likely to achieve great things. Together.

Let's Talk about Culture

Up to this point, you've heard all great things about how we work and our company's values. But here's the thing: it takes more than just having accomplishments and meeting goals to have a winning culture. The word itself means different things to different people. For us, culture is defined as *our shared beliefs, our shared behaviors, and our individual experience.*

You have to have an environment and atmosphere where individuals feel like they're appreciated for what they do. Where they're encouraged to continue doing those good things and therefore are invested in their own work. And that can feel like a tricky balance to strike when you also want every teammate to feel and know you have their best interests at heart.

Ultimately, we want to have a good time and have an environment where collaboration thrives. In fact, that's what we really think is our key to success. If we can have fun while caring for one another and our clients, and do it all with a great attitude, we're not just ahead of the game, but we will own the game, as well. But it's not always easy to make that kind of company culture happen, much less keep it going.

And then there's another key player in all of these, which is our employees. We want people who are passionate, enthusiastic, and involved. That's our definition of the popular phrase, "Employee Engagement." We know a teammate is engaged when they are passionate, enthusiastic, and involved. Now the key part there is "involved," because involved people stay with a company. And in a field like ours where turnover is fairly high, we need those involved folks to stay happy and involved. It's a fine line to balance.

Toeing that line is a struggle but not always for the reasons you think. Sometimes it becomes a problem before the employee even starts.

It's All about the Vibes

When you get two people in a room who really click, the thing that happens between them is often described as vibes. If you've got good vibes, then there's something about you that makes others feel at ease, and bad vibes, well, nobody wants to hang out with you at the company picnic.

But feelings or vibes don't just apply to people. They also key into an organization as a whole. If a company has good vibes, then not only do people want to work there, but it's also seen outwardly as a good place to be or work with. Bad vibes? Well, we've all heard of or been around companies with bad vibes. Nobody wants to be there, and the company's culture turns into a toxic waste dump.

This atmosphere, the one where people feel safe, relaxed, and enjoy what they do, is a big part of a good company culture. It's the kind that we try to promote here at RSi, because we want people to feel good about working here. When you were a teenager, did you ever work at a place you were embarrassed about? One of our current leaders worked at a pizza joint nearby before he came to us and wouldn't tell a soul about it because he felt it was demeaning to work there. We don't want those kinds of vibes here, and we never want our team members to be embarrassed when they sign onto their computers every morning. So we work really hard to create an environment with good vibes only. It's a challenge, but it pays off in the end.

Turnover and Culture

There's this thing we think and talk about a lot, called institutional knowledge. It's the idea that there is this batch of information that a company and its associates possess, and without it, things don't function as well as they could.

Let me put it another way. Do you have siblings? One of my sisters (I can't reveal which one) told me once about how siblings were great because they are the only other people in the world who grew up in the same house with you and know how crazy your parents are. That right there is institutional knowledge, and it's unique to the people who participated in that experience.

This works on an individual level, too. A current leader at RSi was in the management field at this big tech company for years, working on the design side of things. She tells us about how new people would come into the office, full of zeal, and ready to take on the world. They'd say things like, "We need to change this and if we do so, we'll have a higher conversion rate." This leader would then respond, "We did that two years ago and it didn't work." Then she would share all the circumstances and details of the decision and the why and how of it not working.

Was she rude about it? Sometimes, but that's not the point. She knew these things because she was with the company for a long-enough period of time. She had picked up this batch of data unique to her and her organization that others didn't know.

Now imagine working at a place with a high turnover rate. Say, like in the RCM outsourcing industry. That kind of knowledge the leader described above had at her former company disappears into the ether. The person who recommended that thing would have gotten their wish, it would have failed, and two weeks or years later, once they were gone, someone would try it again with the same results. It would be this endless spiral of wasted time and effort.

That, in a nutshell, is something we have to deal with. Because turnover can be excessive in this industry, we have to figure out a way around the problem, so we don't waste time repeating ourselves. What's that phrase about insanity? Oh right, it's trying the same thing again and again and expecting a different result. And if time equals money, then we don't want to waste either.

So how do we solve this problem? It comes in two forms, both of which seem pretty straightforward.

The first part is acceptance. We know we're going to lose a certain amount of employees through turnover. Our company has been hiring people for years, so we have stats on what that looks like—who leaves within the first week, first month, and first year. Oftentimes it doesn't matter how many bonuses or benefits you offer people; they're just going to go, so we have to accept that.

The other part is culture. We have to develop and create a culture that's so awesome that people don't want to leave. It needs to be aggressively positive and give our team members reasons to stay.

I'll give you an example. We noticed at one point that we would hire people several weeks out from when they would actually start. That's kind of the traditional thing, after all. A lot of people want to give their current employers two weeks' notice, so we give them that. Plus, we need time to get them into the system and prepare their computer hardware. No big deal.

It turns out though that between the day we make the offer and the day they're supposed to start, we lose a ton of people. It's a crazy high amount of folks who just decide to bail on the job.

Now that's obviously a problem, but more of one than it may seem on the surface. That's one more employee we need to find, onboard, and get started, which means more time putting up job listings, more time with HR looking at resumes, and IT getting people set up. And not only that, but think about how demoralizing it would be to be an IT or HR person who is constantly trying to get people started just to see them leave before anything even happens. It's horrible.

We needed to come up with a solution, and we came up with kind of a creative one. The day you are hired at RSi, you are assigned an ambassador. Basically, this person becomes your friend on the inside that you didn't know you had. The ambassador's job is to simply stay in touch with you regularly. Like, every other day, regularly. Most of the communication happens via email or text, but phone calls are allowed, too. These communications not only serve to keep the excitement level high, but they also give new teammates a comfort level heading into their first day. They can get lots of questions out of the way as well as a great idea of how the company functions before they ever go through orientation. Finally, we do realize that anyone who found us was likely looking for other opportunities as well. Deploying the ambassador gives us an opportunity to start winning them over and make them feel like a part of the family while fending off any other offers than come through before they officially start.

But turnover doesn't start and end before the job even begins. Once an employee comes in the door (whether it's virtually or in-person), they need to understand that culture. They need to want to be here. Remember, we want everyone to feel, see, and hear who we really are as an organization.

It's why the culture of the company has to be so good. We need to impact people right from day one—day zero, really—and make sure that every day they show up is going to be their best.

Now look, we understand that turnover is going to happen. People find new jobs, don't work out, or just generally want to move on. And we're fine with that. We celebrate any and every person when they get better offers outside of RSi. We know if you bring on great people, other companies will be interested. (If no one else is recruiting any of your people, you might want to reevaluate who you're hiring.) What we do want to minimize is people leaving before they really get started.

The 49ers

Many a book has been written about and by Bill Walsh, the legendary coach of the San Francisco 49ers. Back in the mid-1970s, the 49ers were not doing great. Their record was horrible, and everyone within the organization felt like they had no chance of ever becoming a winning team. In essence, the culture of the team and its organization stunk.

Enter Bill Walsh in 1979 as the new head coach. Anybody in his position would have looked at the team and seen what a mess he had, but instead, this was his opportunity. See, he had a different vision for the team and knew that to make it become what it would eventually be, he had to change the culture into one of excellence, not mediocrity. Turning the team around wasn't going to be easy, but he had a plan.

Everything started with a set of principles. These concepts, which he called the "Standard of Performance," would give people guideposts to follow. They included a focus on teamwork, discipline, and attention to detail. And ultimately, if the team—both on and off the field—followed these principles, he knew they could eventually become the great team he had in his mind.

But the group was still kind of a mess. People weren't working together, and even the city felt like there was no turning back. So Walsh started to emphasize something he believed in very strongly, which was a sense of community and camaraderie within the team. See, he wanted the players to support one another and work toward a common goal, no matter if that was winning the Super Bowl or cleaning up the locker room. Walsh's feeling was if he could build this sense of community within the team, they would overcome whatever adversity lay in front of them and achieve success.

There was a lot of work ahead of him, and since he was such a stickler for details, it wasn't going to be easy. Walsh buried himself in every aspect of the team, from making plays to running operations. It was grueling work, but soon the results would pay off.

Walsh was known for his meticulous attention to detail, and he always wanted to "set the tone." He scripted the first fifteen to twenty-five plays of every game, believing that by starting the game well determined how it would finish. These early successes helped him to fashion a culture of success. Bill was a believer in "leadership by example." He emphasized the importance of preparation, hard work, and attention to detail and expected the same from his players and coaching staff. He was constantly looking to learn and improve. He studied other successful organizations, both in and out of sports, to glean insights that he could apply to his team.

One of Walsh's greatest legacies is the coaching tree he left behind. Many of his assistants went on to become successful head coaches themselves. He believed in mentoring and developing his coaching staff, which fostered loyalty and continuity within the organization.

Finally, and most importantly, Walsh established a culture of excellence by setting high standards and holding everyone, including himself, accountable. Whether it was in practice, in meetings, or during games, the expectation was always to perform at the highest level.

Walsh's ability to motivate and inspire his players was second to none. And while it took some time, the culture within the 49ers organization started to shift. The players saw the Standard of Performance as something attainable and worked hard to meet it. By working together as a team, they became more effective, and, after some stumbles, they began to win.

Football fans know what happened next. The San Francisco 49ers won the Super Bowl in the 1981 season and then went on to win four more times over the course of the next fifteen years. Walsh and his Standard of Performance took the team from a struggling franchise and turned it into a powerhouse in the NFL. But that wasn't all.

Walsh would go on to write three books: *Finding the Winning Edge*, *Building a Champion: On Football and the Making of the 49ers*, and *The Score Takes Care of Itself: My Philosophy of Leadership*. Soon businesses and organizations started to adopt similar principles for their own groups and saw success as a result. This culture of excellence that Walsh created became a model for success in all aspects of life, not just those on the field. It was truly inspirational.

Now take a moment and think about your team's culture. Is it where you think it should be? If not, consider Walsh's approach. Think about instilling purpose and excellence in everyone involved within your organization, just like how Walsh did with the 49ers. If you can figure that out, you will see success.

What Culture Looks Like

Culture is a complex, multiheaded hydra, full of perspectives and angles that change depending on the day. But overall, we have a pretty good picture of what we do and how it works, so let's break some of that down.

We want a harmonious workplace where everyone is treated with dignity and respect. This is a minimum expectation and the price of admission, but there are still some organizations who don't recognize this. We know, because the people who suffered under those regimes often are now working with us.

This means not talking down to people. Not blaming them for things, even if they were complicit. Looking at your peers and seeing them as just that. This ties into the No BCD part of things, right? Because if we're treating everyone fairly, then we're not blaming, complaining, or defending. We're equals; we're taking ownership and responsibility together, and that's important.

We want our people to take pride in their jobs, too. That means from the day someone steps through the doors on their first day, they're going to have fun, they're going to do well, be happy with what they accomplish, and try to grow themselves along the way. We want our folks not only to leave here when they're ready but also be better people than when they started. Maybe they picked up a bunch of skills that help them in life or their career, or it could just be a general maturity that comes with experience. Everyone should be able to improve their strengths and grow as individuals.

This also comes back to teamwork. We're big on really pushing—almost forcing—collaboration around here. This is even more challenging in a remote environment, but we want our folks to work hand in hand, really building confidence in one another and creating something better than any one of us as an individual can do. Ultimately, no one person can do everything for the company, and we're all stronger as a group than as solo artists. In this way everyone becomes closer to one another and accomplishes more as a result.

We've got one another's backs, too. If something happens that's bad, whether it's a client complaint or just a mistake someone made on the floor, other teammates should want to come in and provide support in any capacity possible. They'll lend a hand if necessary or just be there for a literal or figurative shoulder to cry on.

Again, we're a team. If we sync up together, there's nothing that can stop us, whether it's a small goal or a big one. And that's not only part of our culture, but it's burned into our brains. Together, we're stronger.

Of course, it's not all about us. Our culture also promotes a dedication to our clients. Look, we're nothing without them. I don't mean to say that flippantly, but really, we're not doing much other than hanging out and talking around a table without loyal clients to serve. We want to show them how we'll go above and beyond to satisfy their needs and get the best service possible from us. Again, this is why we shy away from calling the relationship with our clients a partnership. It's not. We strive to serve them. It's why we believe it when we say, "We want to be our client's best employee."

This is not always an easy goal to accomplish, which we also understand. Sometimes we have to go the extra mile to figure out what the customer wants and then use our skills to come up with unique and crazy solutions for those problems. Oh, and we have to balance that with producing outstanding outcomes, so, you know, no pressure.

But it's the "going above and beyond" part that's critical to our culture. Lots of companies say they do that, but we want to actually do it. This could require extra time, effort, and/or energy, and we understand that. We just want all of our people to feel like not only should they help our customers but almost should they *need* to do so.

Now do we perform all these tasks in a vacuum? No. We understand how too much work and no play makes Jack want to take a hammer to his temple, so we also push fun and games as part of our culture. Management understands that fundamentally this place can be challenging to work at. We know some of our employees get yelled at on the phone, and that's not a fun place to be. So we compensate that with more fun activities. And we put a premium on being a happy and supportive workplace.

A friend whose wife is a manager at this fancy furniture store told me about the other day when she was yelled at by two different customers. Now when I say "yelled," I don't mean they raised their voices. No, she had multiple people close to screaming at her because they felt they weren't getting what they thought they deserved. It was demeaning, demoralizing, and frustrating.

We don't sell furniture, but we do have people who yell at us on occasion, so we know the feeling. And at RSi, we want the teammates to know we're here for them emotionally, but also there's more fun activities around the corner. And not just the cheesy team bonding kind, either. These are legit good times to be had that may not make those yelling experiences go away completely but at least push them to the back of the mind. We've also proven through our actions that we won't ask any RSi-er to take abuse from anyone—including clients.

Here are just a few examples of the ways we keep our team passionate and motivated:

- Monthly Virtual Staff Meetings full of fun activities, music, recognition, leadership voices, and business information

- Monthly recognition of Employees of the Month, Supervisors of the Month, and DNA Awards opportunities in every department

- Five $1,000 raffle winners drawn each month during the Staff Meeting—based on eligibility

- Bimonthly "Espresso Yourself" informal Teams Video Chats, sometimes on specific topics and sometimes purely a venue for employees across the country to get to know one another

- Unity Meetings for executive-led discussions on Values, Culture, and other topics

- Monthly Virtual Wellness Seminars, each focusing on different issues, reinforcing that we care about the whole person

- Start/Stop/Continue (otherwise known as SSCs) confidential one-on-one forums where members of the Leadership Team engage with employees to elicit feedback and problem-solve

- Book Club monthly virtual dialogue where employees discuss a variety of literature and authors

- Paid time off for hours worked at qualified RSi-led volunteer service events in various markets

- People Ambassador program that pairs new employees with an experienced member of their department offering mentorship and relationship building

- Weekly contest and prizes such as "Name That Tune Friday" and "Trivia Thursday "

Celebrating people's successes is also critical. If you or your team hits a goal, does something amazing, or just nails a call, we want to shout that to the rooftops. We want everyone to feel like they're a part of a team; a community where camaraderie is encouraged. It's critical not only to keeping people here but also to keeping them happy. And we don't want teammates who aren't happy because of something the company isn't doing.

The Harder You Work, the Luckier You Get

Another quick story for you. Meet Joshua. He works in real estate out west. He's got a real go-getter attitude, great marketing program, and just a really solid support system. He sees this guy once every few months that's a bit more than a mentor and maybe even a bit of a psychologist. It's almost a spiritual thing whenever they meet up, which means that Joshua spends the next few weeks thinking about what they discuss.

One day, Joshua came to one of his meetings at the mentor's home a little bit down. The mentor noticed and said, "Hey, what's going on? You seem like you're a bit off today."

It was true, he did look sad. Joshua said, "Remember that big social media plan I had? The one I've worked on and strategized about for the past year? Well, I put it in action, and it's just not playing out the way I thought. I don't know if I'd call it a failure or not, but it's certainly not good."

The mentor sighed. "Sure. That happens sometimes," and then shrugged his shoulders slightly.

Joshua continued, "I guess what frustrates me about the whole thing is that I put a ton of time and effort into the project. It would be one thing if I had done this on the side or half-heartedly, but this was a true labor of love. I felt like I was willing this thing to succeed and it didn't happen." He paused for a moment and thought. Then he said, "It's like I felt I deserved a better outcome and it didn't happen. That sucks."

At that last sentence, the mentor perked up. But before he answered, he deliberated with himself just for a moment. Then, after his beat, he said, "Did you know that I'm a gardener?"

Josh looked at him with a puzzled expression. This was a weird time for a non-sequitur but whatever. "Nope, I had no idea. Thanks for sharing."

"Yeah, absolutely," the mentor responded. "Here, let's go outside real quick and take a look at my garden."

The two got up, strolled outside, and, sure enough, there was this beautiful garden set up in the back of the property. There were these beautifully raised plant beds situated across the back wall with stakes to help the larger plants and vines grow tall. Flowers dotted the sides of the fence, and everything on the surface looked to be like a nice, cohesive piece of work. It was beautiful.

As they strolled across the garden, the mentor started pointing out some of his favorite plants. "That one there is a leek. Ever seen leeks before? They grow pretty well out here, believe it or not." But then they came upon this one patch that wasn't so great. It was almost a blight on the rest of this perfect yard. Here was a blank spot full of rotten something. Joshua couldn't figure it out.

"Oh, that?" the mentor asked. "Those are my strawberries."

Joshua took a closer look, but there wasn't anything red or juicy anywhere in the soil or nearby. Just a lot of dead plant life.

"Yeah, those ones were frustrating. I followed all the right rules, talked to professionals in the field about it, made sure there were no weeds, no bugs, nothing. It was watered, fertilized, and tended for exactly the way every book says to do and planted at just the right time. I was so looking forward to having a salad this summer made with plants from my garden and topped off with these strawberries."

The mentor played with the dead leaves in his hands gently. "But, thing is, they still died."

The mentee, Joshua, saw the disappointment in his mentor's face.

Seeing how his young protégé looked, the mentor turned to face him. "Sure, I did everything right. But no matter how much you want to get the end result, sometimes it doesn't work out that way. All you can do is control the controllable, take responsibility for doing all that you can, and let the rest happen as it happens."

Ah. This was a very "Yoda" moment for Joshua, but it didn't stop him from being frustrated. "So what do I do then? Do I keep pouring my heart into these projects and just accept that they're going to fail? If success isn't guaranteed, do I just give up?"

The mentor chuckled a little bit. "Sure, I mean, that's one option." He continued as the two started to walk back inside, "That's always the problem, right? And it's the one that gives so many people an excuse for not doing anything remarkable with their lives. If you can't be sure you'll ever succeed, why bother?"

Joshua was nodding at this point in agreement and went to sit down at the table, while the mentor was opening up the fridge to grab something for the two of them.

"Oh, can you grab something for me in that cabinet up there?" the mentor asked.

He walked over to the cabinet in question, and as Joshua opened it up, he saw this bowl full of beautiful strawberries. They were bigger than he had ever seen before, dark in color, and looked delicious. As he turned in shock, holding the bowl between his hands, he noticed that his mentor was holding two salad plates. All they were missing were some strawberries.

"So, the thing is, my second crop of strawberries turned out pretty good," the mentor said as he took the bowl from Joshua and started slicing them for the salads. "If you consistently do the right thing, you'll dramatically increase the chances you'll get a good, maybe even phenomenal, outcome." Then he added, "And sure, I could have gotten rid of those dead strawberries, but they're a good reminder of the power of consistency."

The sliced strawberries were then delicately placed onto the salads with care. "But if you give up because you get a few negative results, you'll never reap the rewards." And then the mentor placed the two plates on the table with a pair of forks.

Joshua was shocked but delighted. This was why he had a mentor. This was why he pushed forward every day. "You know, I don't come here for life lessons every month." The mentor looked back at him with a quizzical look. "Really, it's just an opportunity to get a good salad."

STUFF WORTH REMEMBERING

Culture is everything in your company. When you've got a bad one, everyone knows it. And if it's healthy? Well, then you're the place where people want to work.

Building your company culture starts with the DNA of the organization and flows into its values. Those values, the ones I've talked about through this entire book, help you make decisions, particularly about the people you're hiring. Those same folks are going to shape what your culture looks like, so invest in them early and often, and you'll have your best chance at the phenomenal outcome.

Key Questions to Ask to Develop Your Culture

1. Why do we want to develop a winning culture?

   □ This question goes beyond the obvious answer of "to win." What are the underlying motivations and values of the organization? Be real!

2. What does a winning culture look like for our organization specifically, and how will we measure success?

   □ While there are universal elements to a winning culture, what it looks like can vary based on the nature of the organization, its current challenges, industry dynamics, and more. Leaders should have a clear vision of the end goal and be able to articulate it. Having tangible metrics of success is crucial. We use attrition rate, SSC feedback, and employee surveys, but there are an unlimited number of ways to measure.

3. Are we prepared to make difficult decisions and sustain efforts in the long run?

   □ This could mean restructuring teams, parting ways with longtime employees who don't align with the new vision, or investing in long-term initiatives that might not yield immediate results. A big question for the leaders: Are you ready to lead by example?

CHAPTER NINE

PUTTING IT ALL TOGETHER

And, for those who have never owned/operated a business, stuff always goes wrong, constantly. All businesses are loosely functioning disasters that sometimes make money. Those who are successful long-term are able to create redundancies and absorb the inevitable big shocks.

—BRENT BESHORE

In the mid-1980s, a man, we'll call Tom, had been through a tough go of it. He was married, the sole breadwinner for his growing family, and, up until a few years before, everything had been on track. But when his second kid came, everything got thrown all over the place.

That child, a little girl, was sick. Really sick. And now the financial issues were mounting, with medical bills piling up. Tom needed to figure out what he could do to make more money, as his day job wasn't cutting it.

Fortunately, a solution presented itself. It just happened to be in the worst way possible, when Tom was fired. Now he not only needed to figure out an option but do it fast.

Tom had a few friends at the company, and they were also let go and looking for work. Over drinks one night, Tom and two of them came up with a plan. They would either start a company on their own or buy one and fix it. Once the evening was over, they went their separate ways so that they could start off fresh the following morning.

It took a few weeks, but eventually the trio found a company. It sold computer software, which not only did all of them know about, but Tom understood really well. See, Tom did some programming in college on a computer that was the size of a small room and had kept up with the industry. He knew he could make things work, even if it took a little bit of time. The other two agreed, and they pooled their money and purchased the business.

Things went poorly right off the bat. The three of them had done some due diligence but not enough. The company wasn't making money, the product needed some work, and it was going to be difficult to pull themselves out of the skid. One of the three men bailed immediately. He sold his third of the company to the other two, leaving them to pick up the pieces. The next man decided his role was best served as an investor, and so he stepped aside, leaving Tom to figure out how to make the whole thing work.

And, as it turns out, Tom did just that.

For the next ten years, Tom built the business. He never took on outside investors other than the one and, slowly but surely, rode the wave that was the computer revolution all the way to success. He now had a nice office with a growing staff and lots of new work on the horizon. He even made peace with the rest of his group and would regularly meet them for drinks to catch up. Everything was looking good for Tom, or at least it was until he hit a roadblock.

Although Tom did know how to run a business, he realized it was missing something. His company culture was a bit of a mess. It all centered around him and his story, but that wasn't really what the business needed. There had to be some missing piece, but he couldn't quite figure it out.

The original founding trio were still pals, and so, over drinks again, they sat down and talked this through. After messing about with a few ideas, they realized what was missing: purpose.

Employees needed to see what the company stood for, why it existed, why it did what it did, and what it felt was important. The purpose of the company was critical, as were the values.

Tom didn't want to make those changes in a vacuum, so he pulled together key people in the organization aside to ask for their thoughts. Not all of their ideas aligned with his, but in the end, he came up with a purpose statement and a list of values. This combination would get delivered to the entire team in a few different formats, and then he'd see what happened next.

Once everything was out there, Tom sat back and waited. It didn't take long for him to get results. Employees would come to him privately and thank him for including their ideas into the project or express appreciation for creating them in the first place. And while it took a little bit of time, as new employees were onboarded, he started to see a solid improvement in not only engagement but also enthusiasm. The team had purpose now, and as a result, things went smoother. Even though he hated the overused phrase, he often said to himself that everyone seemed "on the same page."

Now was all of his success attributable to the values? Or to the purpose or the culture they came together to define? Nope. But they certainly helped push things in the right direction, and frankly, that's all Tom needed. Sometimes it's the little things that push you across the finish line, and for Tom, this was it.

Maybe it will be for you, too.

Looking at the Audience

A lot of weird things happen when you write a book. See, I started this process with a very specific goal. This book, the one you're holding in your hands (or reading on a screen) right now, was intended to be a training tool. When we hire someone at RSi, this book was going to be one of the things we handed out to them as part of the acceptance package. All of our teammates go through an extensive orientation period, and this book was one of the things they could do in that time window before they got a computer assigned or access to the office.

There was a secondary goal, too. We've got lots of clients, sure. But we have even more potential clients, and having a book that we could toss their way seemed pretty cool to do. It would let them know what we stand for and allow them to figure out quickly and easily if their organization was a fit with ours. That's no small benefit, since most of our relationships are designed for multiple years, not a few months. For our potential clients to know who and what they are getting into would be no small thing.

But a funny thing happened, as cliche as that is to say. As I was hammering out chapters, I realized that there may be another audience built into this whole thing: entrepreneurs launching their first venture. Small business owners who want to take their company to the next level. People who just want to determine their own values and see how a business does it as just another slant on the usual takes. The readers of this book, therefore, don't have to be just people who work for RSi or may do business with us, but other people outside our world, too. The ideas and principles are both universal and basic. They also fall into the "simple, but not easy" category.

This process was not about ego. I didn't (and don't) think writing this book is about me in any way, and so entertaining the idea that it could have a wider appeal than I initially intended seemed like a useless idea. But the more I thought about things, I realized the book is what the book is. And whoever reads it is either going to be affiliated with RSi or not, and maybe some of this is worth sharing outside of our realm.

And so that's where we come to in this, the last chapter before things wrap up. It's a section designed for everyone else not connected to RSi: the new business owners. The folks who love reading about how to improve your company the way I do. The people on the outside looking in.

If you're an RSi-er, thank you for reading this far, but feel free to skip this chapter. For everyone else, let's put this whole thing together.

Let's Start at the Beginning

Say you've got an idea, and you want to build a company around it. Or maybe you're already running a venture, successful or not, and you are trying to take it to the next level. What's the most important thing you need to succeed? The right people. And just like this book, that's where you've got to start, too.

Building or reinforcing your existing team is critical. These folks are going to elevate your company and help you succeed. Sure, you could try to make a go of it yourself, but the facts are, most people who do bring a company to the higher levels do so because they have great teams on board as well.

For us, and you, that starts with how you build the company. The DNA of the team you put together. What we found was determining what kind of people we wanted before we even considered hiring was critical. That's where we came up with our three characteristics:

- sharp

- enthusiastic

- committed

Those are ours, but yours can be whatever you want. You could have three traits or twelve (I'd suggest staying away from higher numbers, though, as that may whittle your pool of potential candidates down to zero).

Let's put this into practice. Say you've got a youth fitness fundraising program. You and your team of people go from elementary school to elementary school, putting on fun runs and other events to help raise money for the institution. Your characteristics could look like this:

- peppy

- energetic

- athletic

This makes sense, right? If you're trying to get kids to go out and run around a track for a few hours, you need to motivate them. Otherwise, you end up with a few of them picking grass in the outfield and one or two planked in the middle of the course. And while "athletic" is a physical trait, it's pretty important here as well. Those kids need to see you do the work too, so they feel like everyone is involved.

Another example: Say you've got a restaurant, and you need to hire cooks, wait staff, dishwashers, and the like. You could want this to be part of your DNA:

- motivated

- professional

- passionate

I could go on here, but you get the gist: Pick a cluster of characteristics that form the DNA of your ideal employees. Then, start hiring people that fit those descriptors.

Like I said early on in the book, this clarity of what kind of employee you want on staff is pretty spectacular when it's enacted. It gives you an idea of what will work and what won't when you're going through résumés or just giving interviews. And for existing employees, you can train them to work toward those characteristics as goals. It works in a bunch of different ways, and it helps to experiment with the process.

Picking Your Core Values

This book has focused primarily on company values, namely, the ones we use here at RSi. Now it's time for you to figure out your own.

You already know why this is important, but just in case it's been a minute since you read that chapter, these are the ideals that shape your company. They're not aspirational; these are actualized concepts that you and your team are living and will live every day. They guide your behavior, inform your decisions, and are the ultimate measure of whether or not you're doing things the way you want your company to be.

Oh, and they're set in stone and nonnegotiable.

But how do you find what values work for you? Well, first off, feel free to crib off our notes. We're not the only company in the world who practices what we do, so take what works for you and what doesn't and see how it fits.

Otherwise, it's time to explore your options. A quick Google search will give you hundreds of different examples, but here are a few I like, which I found at Achievers.com.[8]

From Bayhealth:

- Compassion: We are kind and caring to everyone we encounter.

- Accountability: Each of us is responsible for our words, our actions, and our results.

- Respect: We value everyone and treat people with dignity and professionalism.

- Integrity: We build trust through responsible actions and honest relationships.

- Teamwork: We achieve more when we collaborate and all work together.

Now these are a lot of standard things that you'd see at a lot of places, but for a healthcare company, these make sense.

---

8 Kellie Wong, "Company Core Value Examples," Achievers, September 26, 2023, https://www.achievers.com/blog/company-core-value-examples/#:~:text=Accountability%3A%20Each%20of%20us%20is,collaborate%20and%20all%20work%20together.

From Cox Automotive:[9]

The Why:

- Empower people today to build a better future for the next generation.

The Hows:

- Do the right thing. Always.

- Lead by example.

- Bring out the best in everyone.

- Make a little music.

- Do it all in the spirit of Cox.

The Whats:

- Identify and invest in growth and diversification.

- Delight our customers.

- Honor our commitments.

- Develop and incorporate new technology.

- Improve financial security.

Now what's nice with these is you've got them grouped into pretty standard "What, why, and hows" that are similar to those journalistic rules of "Who, what, where, why, and when." But not only does this give them a lot of options, it also is pretty straightforward. I could make the argument that the "Why" is more of a "What," but that's me nitpicking. Ultimately, you've got a good set of goals right here.

---

9   Cox Enterprises, "Our Purpose," accessed September 26, 2023, https://www.coxenterprises.com/about-us/our-purpose.

Then there's Discover:[10]

- Doing the right thing

- Innovation

- Simplicity

- Collaboration

- Openness

- Volunteerism

- Enthusiasm

- Respect

Again, clear and simple values. They're mostly one-word answers, and they give you a straightforward idea of what the company expects of its employees.

I could continue with lists like this, but let's look at it another way. If you're looking for values for your company, there are tons of ways to find them. See what exists in your organization now. What are the guiding principles today? What makes you potentially great right now? Answering those questions is the starting point. Once those values are established, determine what other values you need to cultivate and how they align to how you're already working. A couple of quick thoughts:

1. Few is better than more. Anything beyond five is simply hard to remember and practice.

2. Think twice about values that should exist already. You'd be hard pressed to find an organization that goes on record as *not* valuing honesty, pride, and excellence, right?

---

10   Discover, "Discover Cares," accessed September 26, 2023, https://www.discover. com/company/corporate-responsibility/discover-cares/.

But whatever you do, find values that work and stick to them. Consistency is the key. As Tim Kight of Focus 3 says, "People feel your attitude, see your actions, and hear your words." Make sure they all are in 100 percent alignment with your values.

Putting Values through a Different Filter

One thing I haven't talked about thus far is filters. For us, the term "filter" refers to values but not forever ones. These are fungible ideas that change and are very much aspirational.

These filters or lenses are goals of sorts; we want to hit these targets and live by these ideals someday, but we know we still have work to do. In our case, we have two:

1. As we grow, we want to become more efficient, have fewer people per revenue dollar, and pay everyone more money.

2. Allocate resources to get the job done 100 percent right from the beginning, and worry about profitability later.

Let's break both of these down real quick.

Number one seems pretty straightforward, and arguably something every company would want to do. We're looking at efficiency here. Let's say that for every one dollar of revenue, we have ten employees. That doesn't seem very efficient, so the goal then is to have less than that number, whatever it happens to be, per one dollar of revenue.

Now there is a world where RSi pockets that extra cash, but that's not how we see it. Instead, we want to pay our employees more money because of their efficient nature as a reward.

This is also a motivational thing for our employees. If they can push a little bit harder collectively, they'll see the results in their paychecks.

Then there's number two. Like any company, sometimes we screw up. Or, more specifically, we put resources in the wrong place or just do so from an ineffective manner. It happens.

But we also have been doing this kind of thing for a while, so it would make sense that we now know things that we didn't know when we were at the beginning of the path. We understand the importance of getting off to a great start. It not only sets the tone for the client relationship with us, but it also gives our teammates great confidence that they can deliver outstanding results. For this reason, we make it a matter of policy to commit extra resources up front to make sure everything is as close to perfect as possible, and then we go to work to exploit the inevitable efficiencies present, and we move forward. This approach has been a huge success for those we serve as clients, for our teammates, and for RSi.

Now these are our two filters, but you will almost certainly have different ones. That's good, but how do you figure out what's best for you? Start with the basic premise: these are goals, but fungible. You can change these midstream without any penalty. Therefore, look at the things you want to improve at your company, and see if those can become filters. If they can, add them to the list. You don't want a small mountain of filters, because this would ultimately break your system. But one to three ain't bad in our book, so give that a shot.

Getting Engaged

Ask any company leader, and you'll learn that employee engagement can be a struggle. By definition, founders have an interest in the company. Sometimes it's purely personal; maybe we began the company ourselves with $1,000 borrowed from our uncle and a few credit cards. Or it could be you're the VP of sales at a one-hundred-year-old business. You, the management person, have more skin in the game than the average employee, and that's part of the challenge.

As hard as it is, employee engagement is a critical piece of a great environment. Some people just want to clock in and clock out, and that's fine. But they also could be doing harm to the company culture with a negative attitude in those hours they're at the office.

So here's how we look at it. We want enthusiasm and involvement. That last one is pretty critical to employee engagement. We want every team member to get in the game and make a play.

What does that look like on the ground? Depends on the player and their role. But the idea is to keep them engaged with the company in some shape or form. Engaged teammates stay with a company. Teammates staying with a company learn more, grow more, and develop into superstars.

As an example, sometimes we'll throw parties as a reward for a particular team action, and occasionally, we'll ask for volunteers to organize it. Those volunteers are actively engaging with the company in a way that makes them and their teammates happy.

Now that's just one method, and there are a billion others you could choose from. Point is, keep your team on the ball and engaged with your organization, and you'll have a happier and more productive team along the way.

Leaders Set the Tone

I have a close friend, Michael, who does graphic design work for this fairly large tech company. He's been there a few years now, and in that time, management has changed dramatically. Lots of folks coming and going, and so it was no surprise when one day his team endured a realignment, and he was assigned a new leader.

The fellow now in charge had a heavy Boston accent, big beard, and always came into the office with a fresh 32 oz. cup of coffee, ready to take on the day. After the boss with the beard settled into the routine, he started to lay down some rules.

He wanted this design team to function more smoothly, and he would tell the group so. But separately, he'd tell Michael that he felt the team was made up of team members who were too young and inexperienced to do what he wanted them to do.

Now this took Michael by surprise. Here's his new boss, Mr. Big Beard, telling him that his coworkers are, for lack of a better word, incapable. On the surface at least, that's not very nice, but it got worse.

There's a meeting about six months into Beard Boss's tenure. Someone makes a comment about a graphic design term called a "widow." I'm not a designer, but Michael tells me it's when a paragraph ends with one word remaining on the last line, so it looks weird. There are a ton of fixes for the problem, and it's pretty basic stuff to figure out.

So this designer makes the "widow" comment and Beard Boss pipes in: "I've got a YouTube video queued up about leading and kerning. You all should watch that."

This was wildly insulting to Michael. *Of course*, he knew what leading and kerning was. This is Designer 101 stuff, not anything groundbreaking. But here Beard Boss was, explaining (in a quite demeaning way) something to his team that all understood. So why was there a widow? It was a rough draft, so it wasn't addressed yet. No big deal. Nothing to be concerned about, and certainly nothing to make a huge issue.

In another meeting, Beard Boss mocks upper management. He tells his team about how the Chief Marketing Officer (CMO) doesn't know what they're doing and how he thinks they're not qualified to do their job. While Michael questioned this position and didn't accept it completely, many of his coworkers began to lose faith in both the CMO and the organization.

Things get real bad when Beard Boss lays off two of the managers, the ones Michael and his friends like and respect for the quality of their work and leadership. A new "lead designer" comes in who mirrors the attitude and approach of Beard Boss. It's at this point that people start leaving the team, and my friend has to consider his options.

Eight months later, Michael gets a call from one of his ex-coworkers. Beard Boss was fired. His behavior and the culture it created had caused almost all of the team to leave, and the people he brought on, while qualified on paper, simply could not work well enough together to do the job.

So why Michael's story? Because it's something we've learned along the way, too.

Leaders drive the culture. Put horrible leaders in place, and your culture is going to go south, too. And quickly.

It's like a math equation: Leaders drive the culture. Culture drives behavior. Behavior drives results. Culture by itself means nothing. It's the behaviors that matter.

Chesterton's Fence

The other day, I learned about a new term: Chesterton's Fence. You probably haven't heard of this principle before, but before you run to Wikipedia, let me define it for you.

Chesterton's Fence is very simple: do not remove a fence until you know why it was put up in the first place.

This leads to a conversation about second-order thinking. Basically, you want to consider the consequences of your decisions, as well as the consequences of those consequences.

Let's expand on that with an example, and in this case, it comes from Farnam Street:[11]

To give a further example, in a classic post from 2009 on his website, serial entrepreneur, Steve Blank, gives an example of a decision he has repeatedly seen in start-ups. They grow to the point where it makes sense to hire a CFO. Eager to make an immediate difference, the new CFO starts looking for ways to cut costs so that they can point to how they're saving the company money. They take a look at the free snacks and sodas offered to employees and calculate how much they cost per year—perhaps a few thousand dollars. It seems like a waste of money, so they decide to do away with free sodas or start charging a few cents for them. After all, they're paying people enough. They can buy their own sodas.

Blank writes that, in his experience, the outcome is always the same. The original employees who helped the company grow initially notice the change and realize things are not how they were before. Of course they can afford to buy their own sodas. But suddenly having to is just an unmissable sign that the company's culture is changing, which can be enough to prompt the most talented people to jump ship. Attempting to save a relatively small amount of money ends up costing far more in employee turnover. The new CFO didn't consider why that fence was up in the first place.

---

11 Farnam Street (blog), "Chesterton's Fence," accessed September 26, 2023, https://fs.blog/chestertons-fence/.

You, as a leader in your organization, need to think about that fence. You have to consider why something is done before you change it, because the results could be catastrophic and really hard to undo.

STUFF WORTH REMEMBERING

As a leader, you have a million different balls that you're juggling. But when it comes to your values, there is nothing more important than clarifying what matters in your team or business.

This effort will take time and exploration and maybe some heated discussion with your leaders. But invest the time, figure out what values exist in your organization and what new values work for you and the organization, and then enact them. The alignment will be well worth it.

Tips for Putting It All Together

1. Define and Align

   - *Organizational DNA:* Understand the inherent qualities that make your organization unique. This could include its strengths, its natural ways of operating, and the innate traits that have historically determined its success. This is often linked to its origins, founders, or pivotal moments in its history.

- *Core Values:* These should be the fundamental beliefs of the organization. Ask yourself, "What are the nonnegotiables? What do we stand by even if it costs us?" These values should be actionable and lived by everyone in the organization.

- *Purpose:* Why does the organization exist beyond just making money? This is its North Star and guides its decision-making. An authentic purpose will resonate with employees and customers alike.

- *Culture:* This is the manifestation of your DNA, core values, and purpose in daily actions, behaviors, and decisions. It's how things are done.

- Once you have clarity on these elements, ensure that they are in alignment. Your core values should support your purpose, and your culture should be a reflection of both.

2. **Engage and Embed**

   - *Engage Leadership:* The top management needs to not just "buy in" but actively drive and live these elements. Their behavior sets the tone.

   - *Employee Involvement:* Engage employees in the process of defining or refining these elements. They should feel a sense of ownership and resonance. Workshops, focus groups, or brainstorming sessions can be used for this purpose.

   - *Communication:* Constantly communicate these elements through different channels—meetings, newsletters, posters, and more. Stories that exemplify these elements can be particularly powerful.

▫ *Integration:* Embed these elements into daily operations. For instance, incorporate them into recruitment processes, performance reviews, training, and reward systems.

3. **Review and Reinforce**

▫ *Regular Check-Ins:* Periodically review how well these elements are being lived in the organization. Surveys, feedback sessions, and town halls can be useful tools.

▫ *Celebrate Successes:* Publicly recognize and reward teams and individuals who exemplify the organization's DNA, core values, purpose, and culture. This not only encourages such behaviors but also offers practical examples to the rest of the organization.

▫ *Adapt and Evolve:* As the organization grows and changes, these elements may need to be revisited and refined. However, even in their evolution, they should remain authentic and true to the organization's essence.

CONCLUSION

At this point you've read this whole book—or maybe skimmed it—and you're looking for me to wrap it all up in a nice little bow so it all seems complete. And sure, I'm going to do that, but I'm going to do it in a similar way to how I've done the rest of the book: with a story.

See, the leadership at RSi and our investors are always on the lookout for opportunities to enhance and expand our services. This may be through internal improvements or externally through an acquisition. The idea here is that if we can continue to round out our product offering, we would be a stronger organization and our clients would benefit. Big plans, big ideas, and the like. All good but not nearly as easy as it sounds.

But let me get specific about the whole thing. Back in 2019, one of the areas we identified that was in need of expansion was Medicaid enrollment. Now why is that? Say you're a forty-two-year-old female named Tina living in Arizona who hasn't worked recently and doesn't have insurance. She has a health scare that sends her to the hospital for an extended stay, and there's no way for her to pay the bill. We, at RSi, give her a call regarding her bill, and she explains there's no way she can pay, and now we're stuck.

Except, thing is, we're not. Tina could be eligible for Medicaid, which is a government-run program that provides insurance for low-income Americans. Functionally, Medicaid looks and acts like your traditional private insurance coverage, but it's provided by the government. If we were able to get Tina Medicaid coverage, she would have a way to pay for the bill, and we would be able to resolve her balance. Tina would be happy, our client would be happy, and we, at RSi, have solved problems for both of them.

Now that's great from a financial perspective, and we get to help people in a major way. By getting them connected with Medicaid, they also become eligible for other state-run programs and get even more benefits. And look, even though our job is collecting money, we're just fine with never talking to Tina again if it means she's getting better.

To be clear, there are more than a handful of companies that provide Medicaid enrollment, and we're not the only ones looking to acquire that kind of business. This leads us into a host of problems, the first and obvious one being money. When one of these companies comes out on the market, the price goes up by a few multiples, and everything turns into a bidding war. Even worse, sometimes the company wasn't really worth it in terms of what they offered and so on.

In an interesting twist, it turns out the company we would buy was already one of our vendors.

Their name is Invicta, and they have two main prongs to their corporation. The first is a technology angle, and it's something we already use them for. Basically, they use custom APIs (that's application programing interface, just in case you need to know) to obtain claim status for patients and identify insurance on self-pay claims.

Other companies use bots to find the same information, but it's not nearly as clean, dependable, and efficient as it is with Invicta.

The other prong to their operation is their work with Medicaid. They're a Medicaid enrollment provider, and their huge advantage here is with availability. See, a lot of those enrollment companies had operations in two, three, or maybe even five states. But Invicta? They could handle the enrollment for Medicaid in all fifty states.

It was a huge opportunity for us, and most people would've just worked out the deal when we discovered there was a match between our service lines. But we had other priorities. We needed to know whether or not Invicta shared our company's values. They didn't need to literally have our core values ready to go like they photocopied it off a poster in the break room (which you already know we would *never* do), but we wanted someone who hit at least the broad strokes. Really, it wasn't as much of a want as it was a need.

At this point you probably understand why we needed that alignment, but let's just break it down a bit further just in case.

You've probably been on a date before, right? Maybe you met that special someone out at a bar, through an app, or just while you were walking your dog. Those first dates can be brutal. You find out real quick if there's a connection, and whether you're conscious of this or not, it's usually because of the values you and they hold.

Buying a business is no different, at least in that sense. Say you take us, this company with a set of values that we live by, and another business that's run with a devil-may-care attitude and a CEO who doesn't even know what their frontline staff do on a day-to-day basis. Think those two are going to get along? Let's put it this way: there's probably not going to be a second date.

That wasn't the case with Invicta. They shared a lot of our values. They're focused on growth, just like us. They value candor and Team over Individual, but they also aren't huge fans of complaining. Furthermore, like us, their leadership started on the front lines and is very active in the work lives of those currently on the forefront of the business.

Much like us, they have an attitude where if they're not having fun, they're not gonna do it. They like solving problems, and they like interacting with people who do, too. So when we talk about core values, that was the fit.

Of course, discovering what Invicta's values were was a whole other thing. We got our executive teams together on multiple occasions just to discuss that very topic. Sometimes they were probing discussions that lasted a decent amount of time, and for others, they were quick questions to see what we could determine from an off-the-cuff perspective. We wanted to put together multiple proof-of-concept scenarios to show that they really do live up to their values. We got references for people at the highest levels and then went down a step and got references for those people as well. In the end, we validated our concerns and determined that yes, Invicta does have similar values to ours and they live up to them. Perfect.

Now that's not all that goes into a successful acquisition. It can be complicated stuff, and if the company being purchased doesn't think it's a good alignment, they could squash the whole thing anyways. In these situations, we go to them and ask what they're looking for. Invicta was pretty straightforward with us. They were a smaller organization, and they knew they would need the resources and support of a larger company to be able to scale and grow the way they wanted. Seems like we're a perfect fit.

Of course, lawyers then get involved, and they start saying some pretty heavy stuff. I heard the word "bloodbath" more than once, and I definitely girded myself for some harsh meetings. Thing is, those arguments and difficult situations never happened. We were both on the same page, and if there were ever any questions or concerns, we hopped on a call and sorted it out. Yes, there were contracts and all that, but sometimes it just comes down to two people talking on the phone and a good alignment in values.

As of this writing, it's been over a year since the acquisition was completed, and things are going really well. We've already seen some of the positive results of the process. We're bringing in new clients, and there's a great reason why: we're now a comprehensive solution.

Here's how it works: You come into a hospital across the country without insurance and needing something done. Invicta has people on the ground in that area who can help them get coverage through Medicaid if they're eligible. If so, they sign them up—they can even do so retroactively—and get the patient covered. RSi isn't even involved here, because we've helped the patient out before they've defaulted on their obligation.

But let's say Invicta doesn't see the patient for one reason or another. The patient isn't able to pay, leading to a call from us to resolve the account. Invicta can come in at that point too and, if the patient is eligible, get them signed up for Medicaid as well. It's a great option for both the patient and the hospital, and everyone goes home healthy and covered.

We can help the patient before they go into debt, and if they do end up in collections, we can potentially get them out just by signing them up for Medicaid. It makes us a very attractive option for hospitals across the United States, which can help both companies grow even further.

There's another thing we haven't discussed though, and that's the people involved in the transaction. No, not the lawyers, but those who are passively a part of the process: employees.

Your average employee might freak out once they hear about a merger or acquisition, especially those who work in a field that could become redundant. For example, say you work in HR and your company gets purchased. Will the new, larger organization need two HR departments? Probably not, so you might think it's time to polish up your résumé.

So in this case, we've kept Invicta as a separate brand within RSi. They're referred to as "Invicta, an RSi company" along the way. That means all employees are still going to do the jobs they were doing before, as were other team members. Remember, we're all about Team over Individual, and this also means we want to keep everyone on board and growing and thriving.

See that's the thing: With this new addition, we're now over seven hundred employees. So all those people coming over from Invicta can not only keep their jobs but also take part in our referral program to bring more folks in. Plus, if they want to switch to the RSi side of things (and vice versa), there are plenty of opportunities afoot. We're a distributed workforce, so whether you're in Houston or Florida or Alabama or Arizona—wherever you are—it doesn't matter. You've got skill sets that will translate in some of the things we're trying to do, so you can be a part of either team and thrive.

You could say this is a happy ending here, what with us bringing Invicta on board to the team, and you're right. But it would never have happened without that alignment of values.

Values are critical for a business to thrive. And I don't mean ones that you pin up on the wall or just pay lip service to. These are values that you live by and set the standards for your organization. It's meant so much to us here at RSi over the years that without them, I'm not sure we'd have ever found ourselves in a place where we could buy Invicta at all.

If you take away one thing from this book, it's this: whether you're a CEO or a person who cleans the bathrooms (or both), if teammates have the same values and share the same goals, success is just a matter of time. With a lot of fun and some great stories along the way.